CORPORATE GOVERNANCE PRACTICES

Author

Dr. J. K. Khetia

FIRST EDITION

LAXMI BOOK PUBLICATION
258/34, Raviwar Peth,
Solapur-413005
Cell: +91 9595359435

Rs: 250/-

CORPORATE GOVERNANCE PRACTICES

Dr. J. K. Khetia

ISBN- 978-1-329-39860-3
Published by,
Laxmi Book Publication,
258/34, Raviwar Peth,
Solapur, Maharashtra, India.

Contact No. : +91 9595 359 435
Website: http://www.isrj.org
Email ID: ayisrj@yahoo.in

DEDICATED TO

MY

RESPECTED

PARENTS

PREFACE

I am pleased to announce that this book **"Corporate Governance Practices"** is very useful for the people who are interested in commercial field. This book is a result of my experience of thinking. I have tried to make this book user friendly, with simple and lucid style and presentation.

I am thankful to all my family members especially my brother 'Mahesh' for the help, motivation and encouragement to publishing this book.

I take this opportunity to express gratitude to my publisher for publishing this book on time.

Dr. Khetiya J. K.

ABOUT THE AUTHOR

Dr. J. K. Khetia has been serving in Shri M. J. Goriya College, Jam-Khambhalia (Gujarat) with responsibility as a Principal and working as a Head, Department of Commerce since last 17 years. He got his UG Degree, PG Degree and Ph.D. Degree from Saurashtra University, Rajkot. He has attended several conferences and seminar international, national and state level and also presented research paper. He is also member of board of studies in commerce and Senate Member of Saurashtra University, Rajkot. He is also got recognition as a Post Graduate Teacher from the Saurashtra University, Rajkot. His many research papers published in state, National and International level journals and Internationally book.

The books deals with the current issues related to new facing of management, Finance and commerce subject.

CONTENT

OVERVIEW OF CORPORATE GOVERNANCE

Corporate Governance in a dynamic capital market is with an ever changing dynamism with new laws, rules and acts introduced periodically. Awareness in this concept has triggered in depth study of ethics and practices which were normally not prevalent in the Corporate World.

Corporate Governance is the heavily discussed buzz word in the Corporate Market. Without it, the company can neither flourish nor prosper. It has become inevitable for existence and survival. When governance has been the key for every successful endeavor, Corporate Governance cannot be ruled out.

Corporate governance – the concept which is the thematic approach of understanding about corporate governance. It highlights the meaning, evolution, elements, factors, structure, its significance, its advantages and its ultimate need in a dynamic capital market. It also highlights the fundamental need of governance which ultimately leads to its acceptance and compulsion in a strategic world.

The historical journey of corporate governance, the basic perspectives, their changes, similarities and otherwise. A specific country wise detail is also noted herein. Models belonging to various countries are compared and contrasted to highlight the fact that no country is without corporate governance practices in a dynamic capital market. India, the country of this study has been given prominent importance and various committees of corporate governance have been studied and compared with those of western countries. The role of the financial regulatory, SEBI has been shown to establish the importance of clause 49. Recent amendments of rules and laws are also shown here to bring out the importance of the ever changing practices in the corporate world.

The ancient roots of corporate governance to enable one to understand the fact that these practices have been incorporated into the country since inception. Further the developments in the various fields of corporate governance are discussed. The role of boards as advisors & monitors of management, corporations & stakeholders, the legal dimensions of board & directors, controlling shareholders, audit committee, bank governance, FICCI & GT survey on corporate governance practices, and the role of ICSI in promoting corporate governance practices are discussed as literature review of corporate governance.

- **CORPORATE GOVERNANCE:**

- **Meaning and Concept of Corporate Governance:**

Governance, this word is derived from the word "gubemare", means to rule or steer. Though originally meant to be a normative framework for exercise of power and acceptance of accountability thereof in the running of kingdoms, reigns and towns, over the years, it has found significant relevance in the corporate world.

The term corporate according to Webster dictionary means a body having the nature of, or acting by means of a corporation. A 'corporation' in turn means a legal entity that exists independently of the persons who have been granted the charter creating it and that is invested with many of the rights given to individual. Applying the concept of governance in the corporate world, what we get is the term "corporate governance". The corporate world comprises of institutions, like companies, firms, proprietorships etc. According to Maw, et al.

(1994), "corporate governance is a topic recently conceived as yet ill-defined and consequently blurred at edges".

Corporate governance is defined as the distribution of rights and responsibilities among different participants in the organization such as the board, managers, shareholders and other stakeholders and spells out rules and procedures for making decisions on corporate affairs.

To conceptualize corporate governance it is important to understand the term governance. The term 'governance' is not word of business but is of political science and nowadays being debated under public administration. Governance is a set of minimum framework of rules necessary to tackle problems guaranteed by a set of institutions. The following are the characteristics of governance when applied in the context of a country:

1. It is the exercise of political, economic and administrative authority in the management of resources.
2. The capacity of governments to design, formulate and implement policies and discharge functions.
3. It comprises mechanisms, processes and institutions through which citizens and groups articulate their interests, exercise their legal rights, meet their obligations and mediate their differences.
4. It includes formal institutions and regimes empowered to enforce compliance, as well as informal arrangements that people and institutions either have agreed to or perceive to be in their interests.

Corporate governance is concerned with establishing a system whereby directors are entrusted with responsibilities and duties in relation to the direction of a company's affair. It is founded on the system of accountability primarily directed towards the shareholders in addition to maximizing shareholders welfare. An effective corporate governance system provides mechanisms for regulating directors' duties in order to restrain them from abusing their powers and to ensure that they act in the best interest of company in broad sense. Corporate governance is also concerned with wider accountability and responsibility of the directors towards other stakeholders on the corporation. These stakeholders include company employees, consumer suppliers, creditors and the wider community.

Sheridan and Kendall have advocated the definition of the term corporate governance (Sheikh and Chatterjee, 2000). They believe that good corporate governance consists a system of structuring, operating and controlling a company in order to achieve the following objectives:

- To fulfill long term strategic goals of the owners, which, may consist of building shareholder value or establishing a dominant market share or maintaining a market lead in a chosen sphere;
- To consider and care for the interest of employees, past, present and future, including planning future needs, recruitment, training and working environment, severance and retirement procedures through to looking after pensioners;
- To maintain good relations with customers and suppliers, in the matters such as quality of service, considerate ordering and account settlement procedures;
- To take account of needs of environment and the local community, in terms of the physical effects of the company's operation on the surrounding area and the economic and cultural interaction with the local population.
- To maintain proper compliance with all the applicable legal and regulatory requirements under which the company is carrying out its activities.

In 1992, the Cadbury Committee on the financial aspects of corporate governance considered inter alia the concept of corporate governance. It defined the concept as the system in which companies are directed and controlled. The board of directors is responsible for the governance of the companies. The shareholders role in governance is to appoint the directors and the auditors to satisfy themselves that an appropriate governance structure is in place.

Zingales (1998) expresses the view that "allocation of ownership, capital structure, managerial incentive schemes, takeovers, board of directors, pressure from institutional investors, product market competition, labour market competition, organisational structure, etc., can all be thought of as institutions that affect the process through which quasi-rents are distributed ". He therefore defines "corporate governance" as "the complex set of constraints that shape the ex-post bargaining over the quasi-rents generated by a firm". Williamson (1985) suggests a similar definition.

Viewing the corporation as a nexus of explicit and implicit contracts, Garvey and Swan (1994) assert that "governance determines how the firm's top decision makers (executives) actually administer such contracts". They also observe that governance only matters when such contracts are incomplete, and that a consequence is that executives "no longer resemble the Marshallian entrepreneur". Shleifer and Vishny (1997) define corporate governance by stating that it "deals with the ways in which suppliers of finance to corporations assure themselves of getting a return on their investment". A similar concept is suggested by Caramanolis- Cotelli (1995), who regards corporate governance as being determined by the equity allocation among insiders (including executives, CEOs, directors or other individual, corporate or institutional investors who are affiliated with management) and outside investors.

John and Senbet (1998) propose the more comprehensive definition that "corporate governance deals with mechanisms by which stakeholders of a corporation exercise control over corporate insiders and management such that their interests are protected". They include as stakeholders notjust shareholders, but also debt holders and even non-financial stakeholders such as employees, suppliers, customers, and other interested parties.

Posthumusa and Solms (2005) quote Sir Adrian Cadbury who defines corporate governance as keeping the balance between economical and social goals and the balance between individuals and communal goals. Furthermore he asserts the aim with corporate governance is to support the interests of individuals, corporations and society (Posthumusa and Solms, 2005).

The IT Governance Institute motivates corporate governance or enterprise governance as they wish to name it, as a set of responsibilities and practices by the board and executive management. The goal with these responsibilities and practices is to provide strategic direction to ensure that objectives are achieved, risks are managed in a correct way and make sure that the enterprise's resources are used accurately (ITGI, 2003).

According to Weill and Ross (2004), OECD defines corporate governance as providing structure for organizational objectives and for monitoring performance to ensure that objectives are attained. Further they mean that there is no single model of good corporate governance. Many countries are interested in a supervisory board which is responsible of protecting the rights of shareholders and stakeholders such as employees, customers etc. (Weill and Ross, 2004).

❖ **Emergence and Importance of Corporate Governance:**

Corporate governance has caught the imagination of all segments of the corporate world. Governance has assumed even greater limelight with the series of corporate failings, both in public and private sectors following with the markets, the investors and the society at large have begun to lose faith in the infallibility of these large systems. At this point of time the conduct of those who take care of the public money is being questioned. They are being tested on minimum ethical standards. They should be questioned as they are the agents of the stakeholders who have invested their money in such corporations.

The seeds of modern corporate governance were probably sown by the Watergate scandal in the US. As a result of subsequent investigations, US regulatory and legislative bodies were able to highlight control failures that had allowed several major corporations to make illegal political contributions and to bribe government officials. This led to the development of the Foreign and Corrupt practices Act, 1977 in USA that contained specific provisions regarding the establishment, maintenance and review of systems of internal control.

This was followed in 1979 by the Securities and Exchange Commission of USA's proposal for mandatory reporting on internal financial controls. In 1985, following a series of high profile business failures in the USA, the most notable one of which being the savings and loan collapse, the Tread Way Commission report was formed. Its primary role was to identify the main causes of misrepresentation in financial reports and to recommend ways of reducing incidence thereof. The Tread Way Commission Report published in 1987 highlighted the need for a proper control environment, independent audit committees and an objective of internal audit function. It is called for published reports on the effectiveness of internal control. It also requested the sponsoring organizations to develop an integrated set of internal control criteria to enable companies to improve their controls. In England, the seeds of modern corporate governance were sown by the Bank of Credit and Commerce International (BCCI) Scandal. The Barings Bank was another landmark. It heightened people's awareness and sensitivity on the issue and resolve that something ought to be done to stem the rot of corporate misdeeds. These couple of examples of corporate failures indicated absence of proper structure and objectives of top management. Corporate governance assumed more importance in light of these corporate failures, which was affecting the shareholders and other interested parties. As a result of these corporate failures and lack of regulatory measurers from authorities as an adequate response to check them in future, the Committee of Sponsoring Organizations (COSO) was born.

The report produced by it in 1992 stipulated a control framework, which has been endorsed and refined in the four subsequent UK reports. Cadbury, Rutte man, Hampel and Turnbull. While developments in the United States stimulated debate in the UK, a spate of scandals and collapses in that country in the late 1980's and early 1990's led shareholders and banks to worry about their investments. These also led the government in UK to recognize that the existing legislation and self-regulation were not working.

The issue of corporate governance became particularly significant in the context of globalization because one special feature of the late 20th century/21st century is that in addition to the traditional three elements of the economy namely physical capital in terms of plant and machinery, technology and labour, the volatile element of financial capital emerged as most challenging part of globalization. Financial capital invested in the emerging markets and in third countries is an important element of modern globalization and has become particularly powerful. Thanks to the ubiquitous application of information technology, at the touch of a computer mouse, it is possible now to transfer billions of dollars across borders. The significance and the impact of the volatility of the financial capital was realized when in June 1997 the currency of South East Asian Countries started melting down in countries like Thailand, Indonesia, South Korea and Malaysia. It was realized by the World Bank and all investors that it is not enough to have good corporate management but one should have also good corporate governance because the investors want to be sure that the decisions taken are ultimately in the interest of all stakeholders. Honesty is the best policy is a fact that is now being re-discovered.

Corporate governance issues became a dominant business topic in the wake of the spate of corporate scandals of midyear 2002—Enron, Worldcom, and Tyco, to name a few. Interest in corporate governance is not new, but the severity of the financial impacts of these scandals undermined the confidence of both the institutional and the individual investor and heightened concerns about the ability and resolve of private enterprises to protect their stakeholders. The scandals and crises are just manifestations of a number of structural reasons why corporate governance has become more important for economic development and a more important policy issue in many countries. First, the private, market-based investment process— underpinned by good corporate governance—is now much more important for most economies than it used to be. Privatization has raised corporate governance issues in sectors that were previously in the hands of the state. Firms have gone to public markets to seek capital, and mutual societies and partnerships have converted themselves into listed corporations. Second, due to technological progress, liberalization and opening up of financial markets, trade liberalization, and other structural reforms—notably, price deregulation and the removal of restrictions on products and ownership—the allocation within and across countries of capital among competing purposes has become more complex, as has monitoring of the use of capital. This makes good governance more important, but also more difficult. Third, the mobilization of capital is increasingly one step removed from the principal- owner, given the increasing size of firms and the growing role of financial intermediaries. The role of institutional investors is growing in many countries, with many economies moving away from "pay as you go" retirement systems. This increased delegation of investment has raised the need for good corporate governance arrangements. Fourth, programs of deregulation and reform have reshaped the local and global financial landscape. Long-standing institutional corporate governance arrangements are being replaced with new institutional arrangements, but in the meantime, inconsistencies and gaps have emerged. Fifth, international financial integration has increased, and trade and investment flows are increasing. This has led to many cross-border issues in corporate governance. Crossborder investment has been increasing, for example, resulting in meetings of corporate governance cultures that are at times uneasy.

In practical terms, corporate governance has meant that there should be at the board level non-official directors who are professionals and who have no conflicting interests and who can particularly operate the two key committees, the ethics committee and the finance committee to see that there is greater transparency in the management of the enterprise. Corporate governance ultimately has to come to mean better transparency in the operations without sacrificing business strategy or business secrets which are necessary for success in the market place and absolutely ethical behavior where the conduct of the company will not only be legal but also ethical.

❖ CORPORATE GOVERN ANCE INITIATIVES IN INDIA:

It is observed that the scale and scope of economic reform and development in India over the past 20 years has been impressive. The country has opened up large parts of its economy and capital markets, and in the process has produced many highly regarded companies in sectors such as information technology, banking, autos, steel and textile manufacturing. These companies are now making their presence felt outside India through global mergers and acquisitions. There have been several major corporate governance initiatives launched in India since the mid-1990s. The first was by the Confederation of Indian Industry (CII), India's largest industry and business association, which came up with the first voluntary code of corporate governance in 1998. The second was by the SEBI, now enshrined as Clause 49 of the listing agreement. The third was the Naresh Chandra Committee, which submitted its report in 2002. The fourth was again by SEBI — the

Narayana Murthy Committee, which also submitted its report in 2002. Based on some of the recommendation of this committee, SEBI revised Clause 49 of the Listing Agreement in August 2003.

In April 1998 the country produced one of the first substantial codes of best practice in corporate governance in Asia. It was published not by a governmental body, a securities regulator or a stock exchange, but by the Confederation of Indian Industries (CII), the country's peak industry body. The following year, the government appointed a committee under the leadership of Kumar Mangalam Birla, Chairman, Aditya Birla Group, to draft India's first national code on corporate governance for listed companies. Many of the committee's recommendations were mandatory, closely aligned to international best practice at the time and set higher governance standards for listed companies than most other jurisdictions in Asia. The Indian Code of Corporate Governance, approved by SEBI in early 2000, was implemented in stages over the following two years and led to changes in stock exchange listing rules, notably the new Clause 49 in the Listing Agreement. Further reforms have been made over the past decade to modernize both company law and securities regulations. The Companies Act, 1956 has been amended several times, in areas such as postal ballots and audit committees, while committees were appointed in 2002 and 2004 to recommend improvements. The latter committee, chaired by Dr J.J Irani, was charged with undertaking a comprehensive review of the 1956 Act and its recommendations led to a rewrite of the law and a new Companies Bill, 2008. In the area of securities regulation, SEBI has made numerous changes in recent years including: revising and strengthening Clause 49 in relation to independent directors and audit committees; revising Clause 41 of the Listing Agreement on interim and annual financial results; and amending other listing rules to protect the interests of minority shareholders, for example in mergers and acquisitions. Not surprisingly, the recent Satyam fraud of late 2008 led to renewed reform efforts by Indian authorities and regulators. SEBI brought out new rules in February 2009 requiring greater disclosure by promoters (i.e., controlling shareholders) of their shareholdings and any pledging of shares to third parties.

An effective regulatory and legal framework is indispensable for the proper and sustained growth of the company. In rapidly changing national and global business environment, it has become necessary that regulation of corporate entities is in tune with the emerging economic trends, encourage good corporate governance and enable protection of the interests of the investors and other stakeholders. Further, due to continuous increase in the complexities of business operation, the forms of corporate organizations are constantly changing. As a result, there is a need for the law to take into account the requirements of different kinds of companies that may exist and seek to provide common principles to which all kinds of companies may refer while devising their corporate governance structure.

The important legislations for regulating the entire corporate structure and for dealing with various aspects of governance in companies are Companies Act, 1956 and Companies Bill, 2004. These laws have been introduced and amended, from time to time, to bring more transparency and accountability in the provisions of corporate governance. That is, corporate laws have been simplified so that they are amenable to clear interpretation and provide a framework that would facilitate faster economic growth.

Secondly, the Securities Contracts (Regulation) Act, 1956, Securities and Exchange Board of India Act, 1992 and Depositories Act, 1996 have been introduced by SEBI, with a view to protect the interests of investors in the securities markets as well as to maintain the standards of corporate governance in the country.

The Ministry of Corporate Affairs (MCA) is the main authority for regulating and promoting efficient, transparent and accountable form of corporate governance in the Indian corporate sector. It is constantly working towards improvement in the legislative framework and administrative set up, so as to enable easy incorporation and exit of the companies, as well as convenient compliance of regulations with transparency and accountability in corporate governance.

- **CORPORATE GOVERNANCE MECHANISM:**

The three key constituents of corporate governance are the board of directors, the shareholders and the management.

- The pivotal role in any system of corporate governance is performed by the **board of directors**. It is accountable to the stakeholders and directs and controls the management. It stewards the company, sets its strategic aim and financial goals and oversees their implementation, puts in place adequate internal controls and periodically reports the activities and progress of the company in a transparent manner to all the stakeholders.
- The **shareholders'** role in corporate governance is to appoint the directors and the auditors and to hold the board accountable for the proper governance of the company by requiring the board to provide them periodically with the requisite information in a transparent fashion, of the activities and progress of the company.
- The responsibility of the **management** is to undertake the management of the company in terms of the direction provided by the board, to put in place adequate control systems and to ensure their operation and to provide information to the board on a timely basis and in a transparent manner to enable the board to monitor the accountability of management to it.

Corporate governance mechanisms and controls are designed to reduce the inefficiencies that arise from moral hazard and adverse selection. For example, to monitor managers' behavior, an independent third party (the external auditor) attests the accuracy of information provided by management to investors. An ideal control system should regulate both motivation and ability.

Internal corporate governance controls monitor activities and then take corrective action to accomplish organisational goals.

Examples include:

- **Monitoring by the board of directors**: The board of directors, with its legal authority to hire, fire and compensate top management, safeguards invested capital. Regular board meetings allow potential problems to be identified, discussed and avoided.
- **Internal control procedures and internal auditors**: Internal control procedures are policies implemented by an entity's board of directors, audit committee, management, and other personnel to provide reasonable assurance of the entity achieving its objectives related to reliable financial reporting, operating efficiency, and compliance with laws and regulations. Internal auditors are personnel within an organization who test the design and implementation of the entity's internal control procedures and the reliability of its financial reporting.
- **Balance of power**: The simplest balance of power is very common; require that the President be a different person from the Treasurer. This application of separation of power is further developed in companies where separate divisions check and balance each other's actions.
- **Remuneration**: Performance-based remuneration is designed to relate some proportion of salary to individual performance. It may be in the form of cash or non-cash payments such as shares and share options, superannuation or other benefits.
- **Monitoring by I agree shareholders** and/or **monitoring by banks and other I agree creditors**: Given their large investment in the firm, these stakeholders have the incentives, combined with the right degree of control and power, to monitor the management.

External Corporate Governance Controls

External corporate governance controls encompass the controls external stakeholders exercise over the organization. Examples include: competition, debt covenants, demand for and assessment of performance information (especially financial statements), government regulations, managerial labour market, media pressure and takeovers.

- **Theories of Corporate Governance:**

Theories of corporate governance undoubtedly assist to understand the role that directors may play in contributing to the performance of the organizations they govern. Literature on corporate governance evidenced numerous theories. However, the three predominant theories in corporate governance research, namely agency theory, stewardship theory, and resource dependence theory can be considered as major landmarks.

- **Agency Theory**

Agency theory is concerned with aligning the interests of owners and managers (Jensen and Meckling, 1976; Stano, 1976; Fama, 1980; Fama and Jensen, 1983) and is based on the premise that there is an inherent conflict between the interests of a firm's owners and its management (Fama and Jensen, 1983). Agency theory is directed at the ubiquitous agency relationship, in which one party (the principal) delegates work to another (the agent), who performs that work. Agency theory is concerned with resolving two problems that can occur in agency relationships. The first is the agency problem that arises when (a) the desires or goals of the principal and agent conflict and (b) it is difficult or expensive for the principle to verify what the agent is actually doing. The problem here is that the principal cannot verify that the agent has behaved appropriately. The second is the problem of risk sharing that arises when the principal and agent have different attitudes towards risk. The problem here is that the principle and the agent may prefer different actions because of the different risk preferences. In agency theory terms, the owners are principals and the managers are agents and there is an agency loss which is the extent to which returns to the residual claimants, the owners, fall below what they would be if the principals, the owners, exercised direct control of the corporation (Jensen and Meckling 1976). Agency theory specifies mechanisms which reduce agency loss (Eisenhardt 1989). These include incentive schemes for managers which reward them financially for maximising shareholder interests.

- **Stewardship Theory**

In contrast to agency theory, stewardship theory posits that managers are essentially trustworthy individuals and so are good stewards of the resources entrusted to them (Donaldson, 1990; Donaldson and Davis, 1991; 1994). The theoretical considerations argue a view of managerial motivation alternative to agency theory and which may be termed stewardship theory (Donaldson 1990a, 1990b; Barney 1990). Since inside (or executive) directors spend their working lives in the company they govern, they understand the businesses better than outside directors and so can make superior decisions (Donaldson, 1990; Donaldson and Davis, 1991; 1994). As a result, proponents of stewardship theory contend that superior corporate performance will be linked to a majority of inside directors as they naturally work to maximize profit for shareholders. In the well-known language of motivation (McGregor, 1960), stewardship theory plays a "Theory Y" view of managers to agency's "Theory X" perspective, arguing that an overemphasis on monitoring is unnecessary for the board to impact on corporate performance.

Stewardship theory is based on two premises; namely, that managers are naturally trustworthy (Donaldson, 1990; Donaldson and Preston, 1995) and/or that agency costs will be minimized as a matter of course, as senior executives are unlikely to disadvantage shareholders for fear of jeopardizing their reputations (Donaldson and Davis, 1994).

Further, even if agency costs are a significant concern to a company and monitoring is necessary, stewardship theorists also hypothesise that outside or independent directors will lack the knowledge, time and resources to monitor management effectively (Donaldson and Davis, 1994). Stewardship theory holds that performance variations arise from whether the structural situation in which the executive is located facilitates effective action by the executive. The issue becomes whether or not the organization structure helps the executive to formulate and implement plans for high corporate performance (Donaldson 1985). Structures will be facilitative of this goal to the extent that they provide clear, consistent role expectations and authorize and empower senior management.

❖ **Resource Dependence Theory**

The third major theory of corporate governance is that of resource dependence, which maintains that the board is an essential link between the firm and the essential resources that it needs to maximise performance (Pfeffer, 1973; Pfeffer and Salancik, 1978). Since resource dependence theory draws from both the sociology and management disciplines (Pettigrew, 1992), there is no universally accepted definition of what is an important resource. Sociologists have tended to concentrate on three distinct types of links, namely the links that a board provides to a nation's business elite (Useem, 1984), access to capital (Mizruchi and Stearns, 1988; Stearns and Mizruchi, 1993), or links to competitors (Mizruchi, 1992 and 1996). In each instance, the researchers make credible arguments that the resource in question is a key determinant of success. Management scholars have tended to take a more generic approach, following the resource based view (RBV) of the firm (Barney, 1991; Wernerfelt, 1984). Researchers such as Hillman, Canella, and Paetzold, (2000) and Palmer and Barber (2001) view the board as a potentially important resource for the corporation, especially in its links with the external environment. In major reviews of the board-performance literature, the ability of the board to link into significant resources is seen as one of its key roles (Zahra and Pearce, 1989; Korac-Kakabadse, Kakabadse and Kourim, 2001).

❖ **Prerequisites' and Constituents' of Good Corporate Governance:**

Today adoption of good corporate governance practices has emerged as an integral element for doing business. It is not only a pre-requisite for facing intense competition for sustainable growth in the emerging global market scenario but is also an embodiment of the parameters of fairness, accountability, disclosures and transparency to maximize value for the stakeholders. Corporate governance is beyond the realm of law. It cannot be regulated by legislation alone. Legislation can only lay down a common framework - the "form" to ensure standards. The "substance" will ultimately determine the credibility and integrity of the process. Substance is inexorably linked to the mindset and ethical standards of management. Studies of corporate governance practices across several countries conducted by the Asian Development Bank, International Monetary Fund, Organization for Economic Cooperation and Development and the World Bank reveal that there is no single model of good corporate governance.

The OECD Code also recognizes that different legal systems, institutional frameworks and traditions across countries have led to the development of a range of different approaches to corporate governance. However, a high degree of priority has been placed on the interests of shareholders, who place their trust in corporations to use their investment funds wisely and effectively is common to all good corporate governance regimes.

Also, irrespective of the model, there are three different forms of corporate responsibilities which all models do respect:

- ❖ **Political responsibilities:** the basic political obligations are abiding by legitimate law; respect for the system of rights and the principles of constitutional state.

- **Social responsibilities:** the corporate ethical responsibilities, which the company understands and promotes either as a community with shared values or as a part of larger community with shared values.
- **Economic responsibilities:** acting in accordance with the logic of competitive markets to earn profits on the basis of innovation and respect for the rights/democracy of the shareholders which can be expressed in terms of managements' obligation as 'maximizing shareholders value'.

In addition, business ethics and corporate awareness of the environmental and societal interest of the communities, within which they operate, can have an impact on the reputation and long-term performance of corporations. The main constituents of good corporate governance are:

- **Role and powers of board:** The foremost requirement of good corporate governance is the clear identification of powers, roles, responsibilities and accountability of the board, CEO and the chairman of the board.
- **Code of conduct:** It is essential that an organization's explicitly prescribed code of conduct is communicated to all stakeholders and is clearly understood by them. There should be some system in place to periodically measure and evaluate the adherence to such code of conduct by each member of the organization.
- **Board independence:** An independent board is essential for sound corporate governance. It means that the board is capable of assessing the performance of managers with an objective perspective. Hence, the majority of board members should be independent of both the management team and any commercial dealings with the company. Such independence ensures the effectiveness of the board in supervising the activities of

management as well as make sure that there are no actual or perceived conflicts of interests.

- **Board skills:** In order to be able to undertake its functions effectively, the board must possess the necessary blend of qualities, skills, knowledge and experience so as to make quality contribution. It includes operational or technical expertise, financial skills, legal skills as well as knowledge of government and regulatory requirements.
- **Management environment:** It includes setting up of clear objectives and appropriate ethical framework, establishing due processes, providing for transparency and clear enunciation of responsibility and accountability, implementing sound business planning, encouraging business risk assessment, having right people and right skill for jobs, establishing clear boundaries for acceptable behaviour, establishing performance evaluation measures and evaluating performance and sufficiently recognizing individual and group contribution.
- **Board appointments:** To ensure that the most competent people are appointed in the board, the board positions must be filled through the process of extensive search. A well defined and open procedure must be in place for reappointments as well as for appointment of new directors.
- **Board induction and training:** It is essential to ensure that directors remain abreast of all development, which are or may impact corporate governance and other related issues.
- **Board meetings:** Board meetings are the forums for board decision making. These meetings enable directors to discharge their responsibilities. The effectiveness of board meetings is dependent on carefully planned agendas and providing relevant papers and materials to directors sufficiently prior to board meetings.

- **Strategy setting:** The objective of the company must be clearly documented in a long term corporate strategy including an annual business plan together with achievable and measurable performance targets and milestones.
    - Business and community obligations: Though the basic activity of a business entity is inherently commercial yet it must also take care of community's obligations. The stakeholders must be informed about the approval by the proposed and ongoing initiatives taken to meet the community obligations.
    - Financial and operation al reporting: The board requires comprehensive, regular, reliable, timely, correct and relevant information in a form and of a quality that is appropriate to discharge its function of monitoring corporate performance.
- **Monitoring the board performance:** The board must monitor and evaluate its combined performance and also that of individual directors at periodic intervals, using key performance indicators besides peer review.
- **Audit committee:** It is inter alia responsible for liaison with management, internal and statutory auditors, reviewing the adequacy of internal control and compliance with significant policies and procedures, reporting to the board on the key issues.
- **Risk management:** Risk is an important element of corporate functioning and governance. There should be a clearly established process of identifying, analysing and treating risks, which could prevent the company from effectively achieving its objectives. The board has the ultimate responsibility for identifying major risks to the organization, setting acceptable levels of risks and ensuring that senior management takes steps to detect, monitor and control these risks.

A good corporate governance recognizes the diverse interests of shareholders, lenders, employees, government, etc. The new concept of governance to bring about quality corporate governance is not only a necessity to serve the divergent corporate interests, but also is a key requirement in the best interest of the corporate themselves and the economy.

❖ OTHER KEY ISSUES IN CORPORATE GOVERNANCE:

1. **Philosophy**: Globalization has increased the competition in which the corporate world operates, therefore, it has become increasingly important for the management to make corporate business more transparent and institutionally sound. Companies are adopting set of practices for achieving their objectives through legal, regulatory and institutional environment. Further, the companies intend to make business practices more and more transparent and accountable for shareholders. For delivering the moral obligations toward society business organizations are emphasizing their governance philosophy.
2. **Efficiency**: Efficiency of any management is judged by the returns generated by it on the shareholder's investment. In developed economies, the capital markets are very organized and small investors invest indirectly, through tax and retirement funds. But in India, institutional as well as individual investors invest in corporations directly. Efficiency issues are pertinent issues as there is no monitoring or control mechanism for the shareholders individually or institutionally through which they can force the management to change their ways to enhance their efficiency levels.
3. **Accountability**: Management act as the interface between corporation and stakeholders. As the interests of various parties as investors, lenders, employees, customers, government and society is at stake, the accountability issues emerge out of their need for more disclosure and transparency in their conduct of business.

4. **Ethical compliance**: Maintaining high ethical standards give considerable advantage to companies as these standards produce "reputation effects" leading to loyalty of clients and customers. Corporate governance and ethical behaviour, together calls for integrity, which is of three types: financial integrity, moral integrity and intellectual integrity.

Corporate governance and ethical behaviour have a number of advantages. Firstly, they help to build good brand image for the company. Once, there is a brand image for the company, there is greater loyalty, once there is greater loyalty, there is greater commitment to the employees and when there is a commitment of employees, the employees will become more creative. In the current competitive environment, creativity is vital to get a competitive edge.

Ethics has got a major role to play in realizing value for the efforts the business organizations put in. Not going anywhere looking from the age old Indian philosophical tradition certain values can be derived, which are also consistent with the value system of other civilizations. They are:

Dharma (righteousness): The right path, which will uphold the family, organizational and the social fabric.

Loka Sangraha (public good): Work not just for private gain but also for public good. Practice of Swartha Pratha (self plus others) seeking one's own gains and also catering to welfare of others,

Kausalam (efficacy): Optimum utilization of resources efficiently and productively. Judicious use of resources and preserving the resources for future generations,

Vividhta (innovation): Beyond survival, business has to be the engine of innovation, constantly seeking more effective solutions to meet economic and social expectations. Such innovation is required in processes, products, materials, machines, organization, strategies, systems and people,

Jigyas a (learning): Change and continuity will co-exist. So the corporate have to keep learning from feedback loop from society and through internal processes of question, challenges, debates and training.

5. **Legal compliance:** A clear and unambiguous legislative and regulatory framework is fundamental to effective corporate governance. The difficulty with legal compliance mechanisms is that many abuses that have enraged the public are entirely legal, for example, companies can file misleading accounting statements that are in complete compliance with Generally Accepted Accounting Principles (GAAP).

Chapter 2

THE CONCEPT OF CORPORATE GOVERNANCE

"Good Corporate Governance is a necessity, and no longer a luxury. Unless a corporation follows the highest degree of transparency and the best principles of Corporate Governance, it will not attract world-class investors. Most importantly, corporations have to be fair to all stakeholders. Sustainable success is not possible otherwise. The need of the hour is to create a climate of opinion which says respect is more important than wealth. It is time to make traditional values like honesty, integrity and decency fashionable again."

– ***N.R. Narayana Murthy, Former Chairman & Chief Mentor, Infosys Technologies Ltd.***

India is the largest democracy in the world, with a population 1.17 billion people as of 2009. Its GDP of $1.209 trillion (2009) has declined in percentage from 9.00% during 07-08 to 6.7% during 08-09. However during 1st Quarter and 2nd Quarter of 2009-10, India has observed the growth rate of 1.8% in GDP (from 6.1% during 1st Quarter to 7.9% during 2nd Quarter of 2009-10).

National Stock Exchange has about 1319 companies listed representing the length, breadth and diversity of the Indian economy which includes from hi-tech to heavy industry, software, refinery, public sector units, and infrastructure to financial services. Listing on NSE raises a company's profile among investors in India and abroad. More importantly, each and every NSE listed company is required to satisfy stringent financial, public distribution and management requirements. High listing standards foster investor confidence and also bring credibility into the stock markets.

Corporate governance is the new buzzword or rather a concept in corporate management that is yet to catch up prominence in India but which has the potential to significantly improve corporate performance. In the case of corporate governance shareholders are considered as ultimate power weilders. Corporate governance has assumed significance in India after it has been given importance by institutions like World Bank, ADB, and Organization for Economic Co-operation and Development (OECD) etc.

A unique feature of the ownership structure of listed companies in India is that, as on March 2009, some **49.81% of equity ownership in 200 companies** constituting the BSE 200 index was held by "promoters" or share owners in operational control. Of the 30 companies on the Bombay Stock Exchange sensitivity index (Sensex) 23 fall in the **'dominant shareholder managed' category**, shareholding ranging from **22% to 90%**. In extending international best practices in corporate governance to countries such as India, it is necessary to appreciate its structural characteristic which can have behavioral influence on issues like board independence, CEO/Chair duality and so on.

This is to imply that there can be or may be certain structural characteristics that can or may have behavioral influence on issues like board independence, CEO/Chair duality, etc. For example, "clause 49 of SEBI guidelines", mandatory for all listed companies, needs to be followed. As per this clause, if the company's chairman is its executive director, then 50% independent directors are required in the total (number of) directors. And if the company's chairman is not its executive director, then 33.33% independent directors are required in the total (number of) directors. So such a structural characteristic will influence board independence. If, for example, the company's chairman is its executive director, he may be in a position to influence decision making.

- **Concept of Governance**

The concept of "governance" is as old as human civilization. Simply stated, "governance" means the process of decision-making and the process by which decisions are implemented (or not implemented). Governance can be used in several contexts such as corporate governance, international governance, national governance and local governance.

Corporate Governance looks at the complete governance of corporations from their very beginning; and in entrepreneurship, through their governance structures, company law, privatization, to their market exit and insolvency. The integrity of corporations, financial institutions and markets is particularly central to the health of our economies and their stability.

"Corporate Governance refers to the processes, mechanism, principles and structure by which the business and affairs of the company are directed, managed and governed effectively. Its goal is to enhance long term shareholder value through improving corporate performance and accountability while taking into account the interest of shareholders."(Swami (Dr.) Parthasarathy, Corporate Governance, Principles, Mechanisms & Practice, 2010)

- **Evolution of Corporate Governance-Illegal Tactics of Indian Corporate**

Pollution control, avoidance of child labour, etc. issues are ways to improve sustainability of operations of corporate, otherwise it disrupts the operation of the company, introduces additional cost, and thereby reduces profitability. An overwhelming large number of Indian corporations use several illegal tactics such as cornering of industrial licenses with a view to keep away competitors, using import licenses to make a quick profit, illegally holding money abroad, indulging in bribery, corruption and other unethical practices with impunity.

High rates of income tax of the 1960's led many companies to devise tax evasion tactics which grew in value over the years, often crossing the lines of legality. Overseas holidays for families shown as business trips, expensive residences shown as office use etc. were relatively common practices for the companies which promised to be honest otherwise.

The net result of such and similar dishonest practices and scams were that the regulators started tightening up especially in the last few years. Also public patience ebbed and intolerance to such issues rose. This fuelled a change in the Indian corporate mindset. These scandals led to the realization that **"Corporate Governance"** was essential and this was advocated by financial press, some financial institutions, and by more enlightened business associations, as well as the regulatory agencies and government.

❖ Meaning of Corporate Governance

Corporate governance is typically perceived by academic literature as dealing with "problems that results from the separation of ownership and control". From this perspective, corporate governance would focus on: the internal structure and rules of the board of directors, the creation of independent audit committees; rules for disclosure of information to shareholders and creditors, and, control of the management. The definition varies according to the analysts, the context of varying degrees of development and from the stand point of academics versus corporate managements. According to one analyst, there is a definite need to eradicate corporate misgovernance and promote corporate governance at all costs. It is not only the stakeholders who are keenly interested in ensuring adoption of best corporate governance practices, but also societies and countries worldwide. Corporate governance is just a set of codes and guidelines to be practiced diligently by companies. India has the Cadbury code and the CII code of desirable corporate governance. These codes generally enjoin corporations to ensure changes in their board structures and procedures with a view to making the company more accountable to shareholders.

- The process of supervision and control intended to ensure that the company's management act in accordance with the interests of shareholders (Parkinson, 1994).
- Not the governance role which is concerned with the running of the business of the company per se , but with giving overall direction to the enterprise, with overseeing and controlling the executive actions of management and with satisfying legitimate expectations of accountability and regulation by interests beyond the corporate boundaries.
- The governance of an enterprise which is the sum of those activities that make up the internal regulation of the business in compliance with the obligations placed on the firm by legislation, ownership and control. It incorporates the trusteeship of assets, their management and their deployment.
- The relationship between shareholders and their companies and the way in which shareholders act to encourage best practice (e.g., by voting at AGMs and by regular meetings with companies' senior management). Increasingly, this includes shareholder 'activism' which involves a campaign by a shareholder or a group of shareholders to achieve change in companies.
- Corporate Governance is consisting of the structures, process, cultures and systems that engender the successful operation of the organization (Keasey and Wright, 1993).

- The system by which companies are directed and controlled (The Cadbury Report, 1992).

Corporate governance involves full set of relationships between a company's management, its board, its shareholders and its stakeholders. Strong corporate governance and capital market's strength decides stability and prosperity as quality governance. In making the legal, institutional and regulatory framework within which governance works, Government plays crucial roles. The efficiency of governance will directly depend on the framework conditions, which would include legal rights of shareholders and its protection strategies.

All the broader vision of corporate governance and the consequent improvements that have been effected in the systems, procedures and the frameworks are the direct outcome of the increasing public awareness about the necessity to have better governance practices. In this effort, not only governments are involved, but are also world-level organizations such as the World Bank, OECD, and Asia Pacific Economic Co-Operation (APEC).

- **Corporate Governance - the concept**
  - **Noble laureate Milton Friedman** defined corporate governance as "the conduct of business in accordance with the shareholders desire, which generally is to make as much money as possible, while conforming to the basic rules of the society embodied in the laws and customs."
  - **Monks and Minow** have defined corporate governance as "Relationships among various participants in determining the direction and performance of a corporation."
  - According to **James D. Wolfenshon,** President of the World Bank, "Corporate Governance is about promoting corporate fairness, transparency and accountability."

- **Standard and Poor's** have defined the corporate governance as "the way a company is organized and managed to ensure that all financial stakeholders (Shareholders and creditors) of the company receive their fair share of a Company's earnings and assets."
- According to **Tricker** "Corporate Governance is concerned with the way corporate entities are governed, as distinct from the way business within those companies are managed. Corporate Governance addresses the issues facing the Board of Directors, such as the interaction with Top Management and relationship with the owners and others interested in the affairs of the Company."
- **OECD** has defined corporate governance to mean, "A system by which business corporations are directed and controlled." ("Principles of Corporate Governance." www.oecd.gov)
- **Cadbury Committee, U.K.** has defined corporate governance: "(It is) the system by which Companies are directed and controlled." It may also be defined as a system of structuring, operating and controlling a company with the following specific aims:
  - Fulfilling long-term strategic goals of Owners.
  - Taking care of the interest of the employees.
  - A consideration for the environment and local community.
  - Maintaining excellent relations with the Customers and Suppliers.
  - Proper Compliance with all applicable legal and regulatory requirements.
- **CII- Desirable Corporate Governance Code** defined the Corporate Governance as: "Corporate Governance deals with the laws, procedures, practices and implicit rules that determine a

Company's ability to take informed managerial decisions vis-à-vis its claimants - in particular, its Shareholders, Creditors, Customers, the State and the employees. There is global consensus about the objective of 'good' corporate governance: maximizing long term shareholders value."(Confederation of Indian Industry, Desirable Corporate Governance, A Code, March 1998)

- **The Kumar Mangalam Birla Committee** constituted by SEBI has observed
- that: "Strong Corporate Governance is indispensable to resilient and vibrant capital markets and is an important instrument of investor protection. It is the blood that fills the veins of transparent corporate disclosures and high quality of accounting practices. It is the muscle that moves viable and accessible financial reporting structure."
- **N.R.Narayana Murthy Committee** on Corporate Governance constituted by SEBI observed that: "Corporate Governance is the acceptance by management of the inalienable rights of the shareholders as the true owners of the corporation and of their own role as trustees on behalf of the shareholders. It is about the commitment values, about ethical business conduct and about making a distinction between personal and corporate funds in the management of the Company."
- **The Institute of Company Secretaries of India** has also defined the term Corporate Governance as: "Corporate Governance is the application of best management practices, compliance of Law in true letter and spirit and adherence to ethical standards for effective management and distribution of wealth and discharge of social responsibility for sustainable development of all stakeholders."

❖ Elements of Good Corporate Governance:

1. Role and Powers of the Board:

The Board as a main functionary is primarily responsible to ensure value creation for its stakeholders. The absence of clearly designated role and powers of the Board weakens accountability mechanism and threatens the achievements of organizational goals.

2. Legislation:

Clear and unambiguous legislation and regulations are fundamental to effective corporate governance. Legislation that requires continuing legal interpretation or is difficult to interpret on a day-to-day basis can be subject to deliberate manipulation or inadvertent misinterpretation.

3. Management Environment:

Management environment includes setting-up of clear objectives and appropriate ethical framework, establishing due process, providing for transparency and clear enunciation of responsibility and accountability.

4. Board Skills:

To be able to undertake its functions efficiently and effectively, the Board must possess the necessary blend of qualities, skills, knowledge and experience. Each of the directors should make quality contribution.

5. Board Appointment:

To ensure that the most competent people are appointed in the Board, the Board positions should be filed through the process of extensive search. A well-defined and open procedure must be in place for reappointment as well as for appointment of new Directors.

6. Board Induction and training:

Directors must have a broad understanding of the area of operation of the Company's business, corporate strategy and challenges being faced by the Board.

7. Board Independence:

Independent Board is essential for sound Corporate Governance. This goal may be achieved by associating sufficient number of independent directors with the Board. Independence of Directors would ensure that there are no actual or perceived conflicts of interests. It also ensures that the Board is effective in supervising and is challenging the activities of management.

8. Board Meeting:

Attending the Board Meeting regularly and preparing thoroughly before entering the Boardroom, increases the quality of interaction at Board Meeting. Board meetings are the forums for Board decision-making. These meetings enable the Directors to discharge their responsibilities meaningfully.

9. Code of Conduct:

It is essential that the organization's explicitly prescribed norms of ethical practices and code of conduct are communicated to all stakeholders and are clearly understood and followed by each member of the organization.

10. Strategy Setting:

The objectives of the organization must be properly documented in a long- term corporate strategy including an annual business plan together with achievable and measurable performance targets and milestones.

11. Business and community obligations:

Though the basic activity of a business entity is inherently commercial yet it must also take care of community's obligations.

Commercial objectives and community service obligations should be clearly documented after approval of the Board.

12. Financial and operational reporting:

The Board requires comprehensive, reliable and timely information which has a quality that is appropriate to discharge its functions of monitoring corporate performance. The information so provided should not be as extensive and detailed as to hamper comprehension of the key issues.

13. Monitoring the Board performance:

The Board must monitor and evaluate its combined performance and also that of individual directors at periodic intervals, using key performance indicators besides peer review.

14. Audit Committee:

The Audit Committee is *inter alia* responsible for liaison with the management, internal and statutory auditors, for reviewing the adequacy of internal control and compliance with significant policies and procedures, and reporting to the Board on the Key issues. The quality of the Audit Committee significantly contributes to the governance of the company.

15. Risk Management:

Risk is an important element of corporate functioning and governance. There should be a clearly established process of identifying, analyzing and treating risks, which could prevent the company from effectively achieving its objectives. It also involves establishing a link between risk-return resourcing priorities.

❖ **The OECD identifies the following Key elements of good corporate governance:**

1. Rights and Obligations of Shareholders:

A corporate governance framework should protect shareholder rights. It should ensure that there is one vote for one share. It should ensure that management provides sufficient and relevant information. It should encourage shareholders to participate in Annual general meeting and vote. Shareholders should able to share in residual profit (dividends). Minority shareholders should be protected. It should ensure financial transparency in the operation of the company.

Obligations of the shareholders is to use their voting rights wisely, however, at times the shareholders are not aware of their rights and as a part of a good corporate body, it becomes the duty of the management to encourage the shareholders to use their rights.

2. Equitable treatment of shareholders:

OECD and APEC have stressed on the point that all shareholders including minority and foreign shareholders should get equitable treatment. All shareholders should have equal opportunity for redressal of their grievances and violation of their rights. Any change in their voting rights should be subject to a vote by shareholders. Directors should disclose any material interests regarding transactions.

3. Role of stakeholders in corporate governance:

OECD recognizes the fact that there are other stakeholders in corporations apart from the shareholders. Apart from dealers, consumers and the government who constitute the stakeholders' group, there are others too who ought to be considered. Banks, bondholders and workers, for example, are important stakeholders in the way in which companies perform and make decisions. For active stakeholder participation, it should be ensured that the stakeholders have access to relevant information.

4. Disclosure and Transparency:

A number of provisions for the disclosure and transparency must be disseminated to those who are entitled for such information. Transparency / disclosure includes disclosure of information on financial / operating results, ownership structure, member of the board of directors and management, quantitative and qualitative matters concerning employees and the stakeholders in the corporation, governance structures and policies, corporate target and prospects and execution of unusual and complex transaction , transactions including derivative products and their level of risks.

5. Responsibilities of the board:

The OECD guidelines explain in detail the functions of the Board in protecting the company, its shareholders and its other stakeholders. These functions would include concerns about the corporate strategy, risks, executive compensation and performance, accounting and reporting systems, monitoring effectiveness and changing them, if needed. Also the guidelines include establishment of rights and responsibilities of managers and directors.

- **Factors influencing Quality of Corporate Governance**
    - Quality of governance primarily depends on the following factors:
    - Integrity of the management.
    - Ability of the Board.
    - Adequacy of the process.
    - Commitment level of individual Board members.
    - Quality of corporate planning.
    - Participation of stakeholders in the management.

The corporate governance framework depends on the legal, regulatory and institutional environment; business ethics and awareness of the environmental and societal interests of the constituencies in which it operates. So far as monitoring of the Corporate Governance is concerned, Creditors, especially Banks play a key role in governance system, and serve as external monitors over Corporate Performance. Employees and other stakeholders also play an important role in contributing to the long term success and performance of the corporation, while the sovereign States provide overall institutional and legal framework for corporate governance.

- **Significance of Corporate Governance – Society at Large**

Corporate Governance depends on the economic and business environment that has been created by public governance in the country. There cannot be good corporate governance if public governance is weak. In the Indian corporate scene, it is clear that unless India inducts global standards, the scope for scams may increase in the years to come. To reduce it to the minimum, there is an urgent need to improve corporate governance in the country. The legal and administrative environment in India provides great scope for corrupt practices in business.

For more than six decades since independence, lack of transparency and financial disclosures, corruption and mismanagement have been accepted as a way of life and taken in an insulated, license-ridden and non-competitive environment. As a result, unless a management which is committed to be honest and which observes the principle of propriety, the atmosphere would be too tempting not to observe good corporate governance in practice.

India should approach the issue of corporate governance not merely from the point of view of the companies act, 1956 or SEBI guidelines or the codes involved out of recommendations of committees such as the Kumar Mangalam Birla Committee or the Rahul Bajaj Committee, but should look at the entire network of various rules and regulations impinging on business so that there is an integrated holistic system, created for ensuring that transparency and good corporate governance prevail. Corporate governance is important to the society because of following reasons:

- It lays down the framework for creating long-term trust between companies and the external providers of capital.

- It improves strategic thinking at the top by inducing independent directors who bring in a wealth of experience and a host of new ideas.
- It rationalizes the management and does monitoring of risks that a firm faces globally.
- It limits the liability of top management and directors by carefully articulating the decision making process.
- It ensures the integrity of the financial reports.
- It helps to provide a degree of confidence that is necessary for the proper funding of a market economy.
- In developing countries where shares of most forms are not actively traded on stock markets, adopting standards for transparency in dealing with investors and creditors will bring benefit to all and also it helps to prevent systemic banking crises.
- With strong corporate governance, the firm provides protection to the minority shareholders which have larger and more liquid capital markets. Studies of countries that have their laws on different legal traditions show that those with weak systems tend to result in most companies being controlled by dominant investors while those with strong systems tend to have a widely dispersed ownership structure.
- Corporate Governance gives proper shape to the market system where market system weak, i.e. it makes market system very strong in the long run.
- Corporate Governance provides transparency in all business transactions.

❖ Benefits of Adoption of Good Corporate Governance Practices

Many large corporations are multinational and / or transnational in nature. This means that these corporations have an impact on citizens of several countries across the globe. It is, therefore, necessary to look at the international scene and examine possible international solutions to corporate governance difficulties. Corporate governance is needed to create a corporate culture of consciousness, transparency and openness. It refers to a combination of laws, rules regulations, procedures and voluntary practices to enable companies to maximize shareholders' long-term value. It should lead to increasing customer satisfaction, shareholder value and wealth. The following are the major benefits for corporations:

- Good corporate governance secures an effective and efficient operation of a company in the interests of all stakeholders. It provides assurance that the management is acting in the best interest of the corporation, thereby contributing to business prosperity through openness in disclosures and accountability.
- Good Corporate Governance creates and enhances competitive advantage for the corporation which facilitates the creation of value for its buyers. It provides innovation strategy to the corporation for managing the process of delivering value. Corporations which develop their strategies by involving all levels of employees create widespread commitment to make the strategies succeed.
- The code of best conduct – policies and procedures governing the behaviour of individuals of a corporation – form part of corporate governance. This enables a corporation to compete more efficiently in the business environment and prevent fraud and malpractices that destroy business from outside.
- Corporate governance is a set of rules that focuses on transparency of information and management accountability. It imposes fiduciary duty on management to act in the best interests of all shareholders and properly disclose operations of the corporations.

- Improved management accountability and operational transparency fulfill investors' expectations and instill confidence on management and corporations, and in return, increase the value of corporation.
- With the development of capital markets and the increasing investment by institutional shareholders and individuals in corporations that are not controlled by particular shareholders, jurisdictions around the world have been developing comprehensive regulatory frameworks to protect the investors. More rules and regulations addressing corporate governance and compliance have been and will be released. Compliance has become a key agenda in establishing good corporate governance. After all, corporate governance ensures the long - term survival of a corporation and thereby enables its shareholders long – term benefits.

❖ Principles and Processes of Corporate Governance

Fundamental principles of Corporate Governance are:

- People Focus
- Formality Organized
- Common Purpose
- Consistent Purpose
- Predictable Performance
- Performance Orientation
- Integrated Development

Corporate Governance should be people focused. All the activities in a business should be planned, organized, executed and controlled keeping people and service to them in mind. This does not mean that the business should be run for charity without earning any profit. No organization can survive without profit but the profit motive should be secondary to the service motive. The company should be formally organized with a definite and clear organization structure. The organization and the people comprising it should work for a common purpose. Journey or consistent flow is life, standstill condition is death, hence the business should possess a consistent process of economic activity. The performance of an organization should be predictable with consistent, sustained and increased growth which reflects the performance orientation and integrated development of the company.

Three "'P's" of corporate governance includes Process management, Process compliances, and Process innovation. The process should be established, integrated, documented, automated, implemented and maintained. Process Management has different aspects such as Organization Management, Resource Management, Supply chain management, Marketing and Brand promotion, Outsourced process management, Environment and Energy management, Relationship management, Information System management, Risk and Crisis management. The plant / unit / organization has to comply with various rules, regulations, statutes and laws enforced by state and central government which includes compliance management , Independent Assurance Mechanism and Whistle Blowing. When certain things are going wrong or violating any norms, rule regulation or any act, the employees should have freedom to sound it off to the top management to take preventive action. (A.C. Fernando, Corporate Governance-Principles, Policies & Practices)

❖ **Theoretical Basis of Corporate Governance**

There are four broad theories to explain and explicate corporate governance:

- Agency Theory
- Stewardship Theory
- Stakeholder Theory
- Sociological Theory

1. **Agency Theory:**

The fundamental theoretical basis of corporate governance is *agency costs.* Shareholders are the owners of any joint stock, limited liability Company, and are the principals of the same.

The management, directly or indirectly selected by the shareholders to pursue such objectives is the *agent.* In many instances, the objectives of managers are at variance from those of the shareholders. For instance, a chief executive may want to increase his managerial empire and personal stature by using the company's funds to finance an unrelated diversification, which could reduce long term shareholder value. Such mismatch of objectives is called *agency problems*.

In agency theory terms, the owners are the principals and managers are the agents and the loss occurring due to mismatch of objectives is called the *agency loss*. The Agency theory specifies the mechanisms which reduce the agency losses. Two broad mechanisms that help reduce agency costs and improve corporate performance through better governance are:

1. **Fair and accurate financial disclosure:** Financial and non-financial disclosures, which relate to the role of the independent, statutory auditors appointed by shareholders to audit a company's accounts should present a fair view of the financial health of the corporation.
2. **Efficient and independent board of directors:** A joint-stock company is owned by the shareholders, who appoint directors to supervise management and ensure that it does all that is necessary legal and ethical means to make the business grow and maximize long-term corporate value. Directors are fiduciaries of the shareholders, not of the management.
3. **Stewardship Theory:** The stewardship theory of corporate governance discounts the possible conflicts between corporate

management & owners and shows a preference for a board of directors made up primarily of corporate insiders. This theory assumes that managers are basically trustworthy and attach significant value to their own personal reputations.

Stewardship theory can be reduced to the following basic concepts:

- The theory defines situations in which managers are not motivated by individual goals, but rather they are stewards whose motives are aligned with the objectives of their principals. (Davis, Schoorman and Donaldson - 1997)
- Given a choice between self-serving behavior and pro-organizational behavior, a steward's behavior will not depart from the interests of his/her organization.
- Control can be potentially counterproductive, because it undermines the pro- organizational behavior of the steward, by lowering his/her motivation.
- The greatest barrier, however, to the adoption of stewardship mechanisms of governance lies in the risk propensity of principals. Risk taking owners will assume that executives are pro-organization and favor stewardship governance mechanisms.

2. Stakeholder Theory:

Stakeholder theory has a lengthy history that dates back to 1930s. The theory represents a synthesis of economics, behavioral science, business ethics and the stakeholder concept. The theory considers the firm as an input-output model by explicitly adding all interest groups – employees, customers, dealers, government and the society at large - to the corporate mix. The theory is often criticized, more often than not as "woolly minded liberalism", mainly because it is not applicable in practice by corporations. Another cause for criticisms is that there is comparatively little empirical evidence to suggest a linkage between stakeholder concept and corporate performance.

The stakeholder model of corporate governance leads to corrupt practices in the hands of managements with a wide option and also to chaos, as it does not differ much from agency model, while increasing exponentially the number of principals the agents have to tackle. (Clive Smallman (2004))

3. Sociological Theory:

The sociological approach to the study of corporate governance has focused mostly on board composition and the implications for power and wealth distribution in society. Problems of interlocking directorships and the concentration of directorships in the hands of a privileged class are viewed as major challenges to equity and social progress. Under this theory, board composition, financial reporting, disclosure and auditing are necessary mechanisms to promote equity and fairness in society.

❖ Need of Corporate Governance

1. Series of scams that shook investor confidence:

The need for corporate governance was first realized in the country with "Big Bull", Harshad Mehta's securities scam that was uncovered in April 1992 involving a large number of banks and resulting in the stock market nose-diving for the first time since the advent of reforms in 1991. This was followed by a sudden growth of cases in 1993 when transnational companies started consolidating their ownership by issuing equity allotments to their respective controlling groups at steep discounts to their market price. In this preferential allotment scam alone, investors lost roughly Rs. 5000 crore.

Another scam took place in 1995-96. Plantation companies scam saw Rs. 50000 crore mopped up from gullible investors who believed plantation schemes would yield huge returns. The so called non-banking finance companies scam that took place in 1995-97 also saw more than Rs.50000 crore mopped up from the public promising them high returns but vanished. The mutual fund scam saw public sector banks rising during 1995-1998 by nearly Rs. 15000 crore by promising huge fixed returns, but all of them flopped. Yet another scandal was the one in which BPL, Sterlite and Videocon price rigging happened with the help of Harshad Mehta. The IT scam during 1999-2000 saw firms change their names to include 'infotech', and investors saw their stocks run away overnight. The year 2001 witnessed yet another scam in which Ketan Parekh resorted to price rigging in association with a bear cartel.

2. Global Concerns:

Fewer concerns are more central to international business and developmental agendas than that of corporate governance. A series of events over the last two decades have placed corporate governance issues as of paramount importance both for the international business community and international financial institutions. Spectacular business failures and serious frauds in the USA as listed earlier, several high profile scandals in Russia and the Asian crisis have brought corporate governance issues to the forefront in developing countries and transition economies. The virtual collapse of the Russian economy in 1998 resulted in large measure from the weakness of governance mechanisms. The consequent distrust predictably resulted in the virtual collapse of external capital of firms; illustrating vividly the fact that corporate misgovernance can shake the very foundations of a society, affecting every member there from. Further, national business communities are gradually realizing the fact that there is no substitute for getting the basic business and management systems in place in order to be competitive in the globe market and to attract foreign investment.

3. America's Hall of Shame-2002:

WorldCom improperly booked $3.8 billion in expenses, thus inflating profits. The founder, Bernie Ebbers, borrowed $208 million from the phone company to cover personal debts. Energy firm, **Ernon**, created outside partnerships that helped hide its poor financial condition. Executives earned millions selling company stocks.

Energy Company, **Dygeny**, was under investigation for accounting and trading malpractices, in part related to California power crisis. **Adelphia Communications** made illegal loans to founder Rigas' family members and was under investigation for accounting malpractices.

The Bush Federal Administration was prompt to slap the punitive measures on erring corporate and preventive steps to avoid future corporate frauds. A new law came into force, known as Sarbanes-Oxley Act, stipulates that CEO's and CFO's will be held completely liable for any criminal and civil suits for any omissions, false statements and restatements.

The history of the development of Indian corporate laws has been marked by interesting contrasts. At independence, India inherited one of the world's poorest economies but one which had well functioning stock markets with clearly defined rules governing listing, trading and settlements; a well-developed equity culture if only among the urban rich; and a banking system replete with well-developed lending norms and recovery procedures. In terms of corporate laws and financial system, therefore, India emerged far better endowed than most other colonies.

The beginning of corporate developments in India were marked by the managing agency system that contributed to the birth of dispersed equity ownership but also gave rise to the practice of management enjoying control rights disproportionately greater than their stock ownership. The turn towards socialism in the decades after independence marked by the 1951 Industries (Development and Regulation) Act as well as the 1956 Industrial Policy Resolution put in place a regime and culture of licensing, protection and widespread red-tape that bred corruption and affected the growth of the corporate sector. The situation grew from bad to worse in the following decades and corruption, favoritism and inefficiency became the hallmarks of the Indian corporate sector. Exorbitant tax rates encouraged creative accounting practices and complicated emolument structures to beat the system.

While the Companies Act provides clear instructions for maintaining and updating share registers, in reality minority shareholders have often suffered from irregularities in share transfers and registrations – deliberate or unintentional. Sometimes non-voting preferential shares have been used by promoters to channel funds and deprive minority shareholders of their dues. Minority shareholders have sometimes been defrauded by the management undertaking clandestine side deals with the acquirers in the relatively scarce event of corporate takeovers and mergers. Boards of directors have been largely ineffective in India in monitoring the actions of management. They are routinely crammed with friends and allies of the promoters and managers, in deliberate violation of the spirit of corporate law. The nominee directors from the Development Financial Institutes, who could and should have played a particularly important role, have usually been incompetent or unwilling to step up to the act. Consequently, the boards of directors have largely functioned as rubber stamps of the management. With the increasing power of the capital market, to discipline the dominant shareholder, by denying him access to the capital market. The newly unleashed forces of deregulation, disintermediation, institutionalization, globalization and tax reforms are making the minority shareholder more powerful and are forcing the companies to adopt healthier governance practices. These trends are expected to become even stronger in future. Regulators can facilitate the process by measures such as enhancing the scope, frequency, quality and reliability of information disclosures; promoting an efficient market for corporate control; restructuring or privatizing the large public sector institutional investors; and reforming bankruptcy and related laws.

A remarkable transformation has been seen in the countries after scams rocking their economies. Not only India but developed countries like US and UK are also not untouched by such scams. Enron or Satyam, both reflect the weakness with the corporate governance and its implementation practices at the ground levels. Capital Markets exerts an influential role on companies by imposing certain rules and regulations relating to firm's governance roles. Being the center of spectrum, which ranges from companies or firms to that of economies, capital markets not only play a major role in but also impart some forces on both the sides. These forces are again functions of governance practices. To reframe or understand the spectrum of fields of corporate governance, it becomes important to focus on listed companies in capital markets and then study the impact of it on both low frequencies to high frequency ends i.e. companies to country.

But a demarcating line is drawn in impression regarding the developed economies and their governance practices and that of emerging companies which are on transitional stage. Since these economies would be developed in future, this transitional era becomes important to lay their foundations which do not blow out the future of governance practices. Contrast between such economies would suggest where emerging economies and their capital markets need reformation over the certain era of development.

Recapitulating, the key to better corporate governance in India today lies in a more efficient and dynamic capital market. Of course, things could change in future if Indian corporate structures also approach the Anglo-American pattern of near complete separation of management and ownership.

Chapter 3

HISTORICAL PERSPECTIVE OF CORPORATE GOVERNANCE

"Over the last decade or so, Corporate Governance has come to acquire an increasingly important place in the conduct of the corporate sector globally. This is understandable considering the expanded role of the corporate sector not just in creating wealth but even in many societal issues, all of which necessitates that society places a higher degree of trust in the same corporates. Thus we have seen several bodies, internationally and nationally engage with the issue of what comprises good Corporate Governance and through the efforts of these bodies, we now have a rich and growing body of the do's and don'ts on the issue."

– Ratan N. Tata, Chairman, Tata Group.

Different countries' economics are organized in very different ways, decisions about how capital is allocated is different and this is the very reason different countries have different paths to follow the corporate governance. The history of adapting the path to follow and implement corporate governance in different countries like, The United States, The United Kingdom, Germany, Japan, China and India are different.

❖ History of Corporate Governance across the World

❖ United States of America (USA):

In 1930's, a remarkable democratization of shareholding took place between the period of World War I and the end of World War II. The benefits of democratization and diversification depend on the depth of the stock market. Popular magazines on share ownership, and popular media coverage of Wall-Street celebrities brought Middle American wealth into the stock market, vastly deepening it and thus making the sacrifice of diversification for control more attractive than elsewhere.

America's response to the Great Depression then razed much of what family capitalism remained. Two great pyramids, the Insull and Van Sweringen business groups, collapsed after the 1929 crash. These high profile collapses appear to have linked to the Depression with highly concentrated corporate control in the public mind, justifying a barrage of progressive reforms. A series of regulatory reforms governing banks, insurance companies, mutual funds and pension funds prevented any of these organizations from accumulating any serious corporate governance influence as per 1937 data on block holding in the top listed 200 US firms.

Although the hostile takeovers of the 1980s disrupted this arrangement for some forms, and some United States institutional investors were clearing their throats, this situation has kept most American firms freestanding and professionally run ever since. Since then, corporate governance has been implemented in most of the companies.

❖ United Kingdom (UK):

Comparison of the firms founded in 1900 to another founded in 1960 has been done in one of the studies conducted. (Monks & Minow, 2008) It is found that ownership grows diffuse in both sets of firms at roughly the same rate. Based on this, an argument is made that the forces that made founding families withdraw from corporate governance in the modern United Kingdom also operated a century ago. Adding to this, a discussion concludes that shareholder rights in the United Kingdom were extremely weak until the later part of the 20th century, and shareholder legal protection permits diffuse ownership in the UK.

Providing a descriptive summary of UK corporate governance in greater generality, the pyramids gained importance at the middle of the century. The corporate disclosure, implemented in 1948, made hostile takeovers less risky for raiders, and that pyramids developed as a defense against hostile takeovers. However, they propose that British corporate insiders were and are governed by higher standards of ethical conduct, which preclude the extraction of such private benefits. Given this, British corporate insiders were more readily convinced to sell their control blocks and dismantle their pyramids. Thus, the current diffuse ownership of British corporations came to prevail early in the 20th century and still persists.

❖ **Germany:**

Fohlin (2004) argues that Germany's large universal banks were less important to its history of corporate governance than is commonly believed. German industrialization advanced rapidly in the late 19th century, financed by wealthy merchant families, foreign investors, small shareholders and private banks, industrial firms with bankers on their boards did not perform better than other firms. German corporate governance appears to be thoughtfully developed in this era. The company law of 1870 created the current dual board structure to protect small shareholders and public from self–serving insiders. It also required uniformity and consistency in accounting, reporting and governance.

The modern German economy thus consists primarily of family controlled pyramidal groups and nominally widely held firms that are actually controlled by the top few banks via proxies. The leading banks collectively also control dominant blocks of own shares. In more recent times, the advantages available to German companies have become 'disadvantages' as they have not been able to attract capital from Institutional Investors in global markets, due to 'parochial governance practices that have obstructed share holders rights'. (Monks and Minow (2001))

❖ **Japan:**

The history of corporate governance in Japan is more complicated and variegated than in any other major country. Prior to 1868, Japan was a deeply conservative and isolationist country. Business families were at the bottom of a hereditary caste system – beneath priests, warriors, peasants, and craftsmen. Unsurprisingly, this moral inversion led to stagnation. Yet the necessity of running a densely populous country forced Japan's feudal shoguns to give prominent mercantile families, like the Mistui and Sumitomo, steadily a greater influence. Japan fell traditionally into the insider-dominated groups and had a 'credit-based financial system (Zysman, 1983) as the economy was characterized by intercompany shareholdings, intercompany directorships and frequently substantial bank involvement.

Recently, the trend has been toward a more market- dominated Japanese system of corporate governance. (Cooke and Sawa, 1998)

These groups, called zaibatsu, were family controlled pyramids of listed corporations, much like those found elsewhere in the world. Later, other groups like Nissan, a pyramidal business group with a widely held firm at its apex, joined in as Japan's economy roared into the 20th century. Thus Japan began its industrialization with a mixture of family and state capitalism. Shareholders eagerly bought shares, especially in numerous subsidiaries floated by these great business groups.

❖ **China:**

Chinese corporate governance in the late 19th and early 20th centuries is of interest because it corresponds to the beginning of china's industrialization and sees the attempted transplanting of western institutions into a nonwestern economy. Pre-communist China's industrial development may thus offer more interesting lessons for modern emerging economies than does post-communist China herself , pre-revolutionary capitalism also provides a model of " a market economy with Chinese characteristics."

Portfolio investors, unable to influence corporate governance after this fact, stayed out of stocks. This kept the Chinese stock market illiquid and subject to severe boom and bust cycles. This, in turn, kept insiders from selling out and diversifying, underscoring the value of their private benefits of control.

❖ **India:**

The fundamentals of Corporate Governance have its deep roots in Indian History. But surprisingly it is very less known to us. Our own ancient texts have laid down sound principles of governance which seem very relevant to modern day corporate requirements.

Years back in 1600, The East India Company was arguably the first to be chartered as a Company by the then Queen Elizabeth I, with a monopoly of trade between England and Far East. Since then, corporations have come a long way, both in terms of their power and wealth-creating potentials, and of institutionalized checks and balances to ensure their sound operations within their mandates and transparent reporting back to the shareholders. Since then the Corporate Governance has become the crucial issue in the Corporate World. Different countries across the World follow different Corporate Governance Systems. India also follows more or less the UK Model of Corporate Governance.

❖ Models of corporate governance

- ❖ The Board of Directors seldom appears on the management organization chart yet it is the ultimate decision making body in a Company. The role of management is to run the enterprise while the role of the board is to see that it is being run well and that too in the right direction.
- ❖ A useful way of depicting the interaction between management and the board is to present the board as a circle superimposed on the hierarchical triangle of management. This model can be applied to the governance of any corporate entity, private or public, profit oriented or service based organization. The circle and Triangle model is a powerful analytical tool. (A.C. Fernando (2009))

Corporate Governance System varies around the World. Scholars tend to suggest three broad versions:

- ❖ The Anglo-American Model;
- ❖ The German Model;
- ❖ The Japanese Model.

This is also known as **unitary board model,** in which all directors participate in a single board comprising both executive and non-executive directors in varying proportions. This approach to governance tends to be shareholder-oriented. The major features of the Anglo-American or Anglo-saxon model of the corporate governance are as follows:

- ❖ The ownership of companies is more or less equally divided between individual shareholders and institutional shareholders.
- ❖ Directors are rarely independent of management.
- ❖ Companies are typically run by professional managers who have negligible ownership stakes. There is a fairly clear separation of ownership and management.

- Most institutional investors are reluctant for certain activities. They view themselves as portfolio investors interested in investing in a broadly diversified portfolio of liquid securities. If they are not satisfied with a company's performance, they simply sell the securities in the market and quit.
- The disclosure norms are comprehensive, the rules against insider trading are tight, and the penalties for price manipulations stiff, all of which provide adequate protection to the small investor and promote general market liquidity. Incidentally, they also discourage large investors from taking an active role in corporate governance.

The Indian companies are governed by the Company's Act of 1956 which follows more or less the UK model. The pattern of private companies is mostly that of closely held or dominated by a founder, his family and associates. India has adopted the key tenants of the Anglo-American external and internal control mechanism after economic liberalization.

The structure and processes of corporate governance are not universally same in all countries. Different countries have adopted different structure and processes in governing their companies depending on suitability of their socio-culture, economic environment, government policy, capital and money market systems etc. Whatever structures of corporate governance are adopted, one thing is common that the board of directors has been reorganized as the heart of the structure of corporate governance and the board processes have been accepted as the most important processes of governance. It has also been reorganized that along with the board of directors, the other participants, viz. shareholders including institutional investors or large shareholders, other stakeholders, banks and auditors etc. do have significant roles in the governance structures and their commitments in the processes of corporate governance. Therefore, while discussing the various structures and processes of corporate governance, it will be prudent to touch upon the roles and commitments of these participants simultaneously, without which the discussion on governance structures and processes remains incomplete. (Vasudha Joshi (2004), Jayanti and Subrate Sarkar, (September 2000))

- **Recommendations of various international committees on Corporate Governance**

- **The Cadbury Committee:**

In December 1992, the Cadbury Committee published the *Code of Best Practice* which recommended that boards of publicly-traded UK corporations include at least three outside directors and that the positions of the chairman of the board and chief executive officer not be held by a single individual. The underlying presumption was that these government-sponsored recommendations would lead to enhanced board oversight. As a test of presumption, corporate analyzes the relation between top management turnover and its performance. Corporate finds that CEO turnover increased following publications of the Code, that the relationship between CEO turnover and performance was strengthened following publication of the Code, and that the increase in the sensitivity of turnover to performance was concentrated among firms that adopted the Cadbury Committee's recommendations. (Jay Dahya, John McConnell and Nickolaos Travlos, The Athens Laboratory of Business Administration, 2000)

The Cadbury Committee was appointed by the Conservative Government of the United Kingdom (UK) in May 1991 with a broad mandate to "address the financial aspects of corporate governance". In December 1992, the Committee issued its report which recommended, among other things, that board of directors of publicly traded companies include at least three non-executive (i.e., outside) directors as members and that the positions of Chairman of the Board (Chairman) and Chief Executive Officer (CEO) of these companies be held by two different individuals. The apparent reasoning underlying the Committee's recommendations is that greater independence of a corporate board will improve the quality of board oversight.

To appreciate the potential significance of the Cadbury Committee and its recommendations, it is important to appreciate the environment surrounding the establishment of the Committee. First, the Committee was appointed in the aftermath of the "scandalous" collapse of several prominent UK companies during the later 1980s and early 1990s, including Ferranti International PLC, Colorol Group, Pollypeck International PLC, Bank of Credit and Commerce International (BCCI) and Maxwell Communication Corporation. The broadsheet press popularly attributed these failures and others to weak governance systems, lax board oversight, and the vesting of control in the hands of a single top executive. (Cadbury Committee Report, 1992)

❖ **The Greenbury Committee, 1995**

This committee was set up in January, 1995 to identify the good practices by the Confederation of British Industry (CBI), in determining directors' remuneration and to prepare a code of such practices for use by public limited companies of United Kingdom.

The Committee mainly focused on the following issues

- ❖ Accountability and level of Directors' pay.
- ❖ Proper reporting to shareholders and greater transparency in the Process.

The Committee produced the Greenbury Code of Best Practice which was divided into following four sections:

- ❖ Remuneration Committee.
- ❖ Disclosures.
- ❖ Remuneration policy.
- ❖ Service Contracts and compensation.

(Greenbury Committee Report (1994), investigating board members' remuneration and responsibilities)

❖ **The Hampel Committee, 1995**

The Hampel Committee was set up in November, 1995 to promote high standards of corporate governance both to protect investors and to preserve and enhance the standing of companies listed on the London Stock Exchange. The committee further developed the Cadbury Committee Report and recommended that:

- ❖ The auditors should report on internal control privately.
- ❖ The directors maintain and review all controls.
- ❖ Companies that do not already have an Internal Audit Function should from time to time review their need for one.

The Committee also introduced the Combined Code that consolidated the recommendation of earlier corporate governance. (Cadbury and Greenbury).

(The Hample Committee Report 1998)

❖ **The Combined Code, 1998**

The Combined Code was subsequently derived from Ron Hampel Committee's Final Report, Cadbury and the Greenbury Report.

- ❖ The stipulations contained in the Combined Code require, among the other things, that the Board should maintain a sound system of internal control to safeguard shareholders' investment and the Companies' assets.
- ❖ It was observed by this committee that the one common denominator behind the past failures in the corporate world was the lack of effective risk management.

❖ **The Turbnell Committee, 1999**

The Turnbell Committee was set up by The Institute of Chartered Accountant in England and Wales (ICAEW) in 1999 to provide guidance to assist companies in implementing the requirements of the Combined Code relating to internal control.

- The Committee recommended that where companies do not have any internal audit function; the board should consider the need for carrying out an internal audit function.
- The Committee also recommended that the board of directors should confirm the existence of procedures for evaluating and managing the key risks.
- According to this Committee, Corporate Governance is not a static concept, in fact it is dynamic, and thus needs to alter with the changes that occur in a business environment. (The Turnbull Committee Report 1998)

- **Sarbanes-Oxley Act, 2002**

Sarbanes-Oxley Act is one which codifies certain standards of good governance as specific requirement.

- The Act calls for protection to those who have the courage to bring frauds to the attention of the authority that has to handle frauds.
- The Sarbanes-Oxley Act (SOX ACT), 2002 is a sincere attempt to address all the issues associated with corporate failures to achieve quality governance and to restore investors' confidence.
- The Act was formulated to protect investors by improving the accuracy and reliability of corporate disclosures, made precious to the securities laws and for other purposes. The Act contains a number of provisions that dramatically change the reporting and corporate director's governance obligations of public companies, the directors and officers. (Cynthia A. Glassman, Commissioner, SEC)

- **Indian Committees and their Guidelines**

Some major committees for corporate governance in India are:

- **Kumar Mangalam Birla Committee, 1999:**
    - The Birla Committee's recommendations consists of mandatory recommendations, and non-mandatory recommendations.
    - Mandatory recommendation includes composition of Board of director and audit committee, remuneration committee of the board procedure of board, management or manner of implementation.
    - Non-mandatory recommendations includes role of the chairman, policy of remuneration committee, rights of shareholders, postal ballot procedure etc. (The Chartered Secretary, March 2000)
- **Nareshchandra Committee Report, 2002**

The Naresh Chandra Committee was appointed as a high-level committee to examine various corporate governance issues by the Department of Company Affairs on 21 August 2002. Naresh Chandra Committee report on 'corporate Audit & Governance' has taken forward the recommendations of the Kumar Mangalam Birla Committee on corporate governance which was set up by the Securities Exchange Board of India on the following counts:

- Representation of independent directors on a company's board.
- The composition of the audit committee.

The Naresh Chandra Committee has laid down stringent guidelines defining the relationship between auditors and their clients. In a move that could impact small audit firms, the committee has recommended that along with its subsidiary, associates or affiliated entities, an audit firm should not derive more than 25 per cent of its business from a single corporate client.

The Committee has further recommended the following:

- Tightening of the noose around the auditors by asking them to make an array of disclosures.
- Calling upon CEOs and CFOs of all listing companies to certify their companies' annual accounts, besides suggesting.
- Setting up of quality review boards by the Institute of Chartered

Accountants of India (ICAI), Institute of Company Secretaries of India (ICSI) and Institute of Cost and Works Accountants of India, instead of a Public oversight board similar to the one in USA.

- **Narayana Murthy Committee Report, 2003**

Under the committee on corporate governance set up by SEBI under N. R. Narayana Murthy, the terms of references were:

- to review the performance of corporate governance and
- to determine the role of companies in responding to rumor and other price sensitive information circulating in the market.

The committee report expresses its total concurrence with the recommendations contained in the Naresh Chandra Committee's report on the following counts:

- Disclosure of contingent liability
- Certification by CEO's and CFO's
- Definition of independent directors
- Independence of Audit committees

The committee came out with two sets of recommendations **namely**, mandatory recommendation and non-mandatory recommendations.

Mandatory recommendation includes composition of audit committee, related party transactions, Proceeds from initials public offerings, risk management code of conduct for the Board or appointment of Nominee directors etc.

Non-mandatory recommendation pertains to moving to a regime providing for unqualified corporate financial statements, training of board members and evaluation of non-executive director's performance by a peer group comprising the entire board of directors, excluding the director being evaluated.

- **Dr. J. J. Irani Committee Report on Company Law, 2005**

The Government of India constituted an expert committee on Company Law on 2 December 2004, under the chairmanship of Dr. J. J. Irani. Set up to structurally evaluate the views of several stakeholders in the development of the Company Law in India in respect of the concept paper promulgated by the union ministry of company affairs , the J. J. Irani Committee has come out with suggestions that will go a long way in laying sound base for corporate growth in the coming years. The main features of its recommendations pertaining to corporate governance are as follows:

- Number of Directors & their duration in company
- Age of Directors
- 1/3rd of Independent Directors (along with definition of Independent Director)
- Maximum No. of Directorship hold by Individual
- Remuneration Policy
- Sitting Fee Structure for Directors
- Requisite Board Meetings in a year
- Number of Independent Directors in Audit Committee
- Constitution of Remuneration Committee
- Protections of Minority shareholders rights
- Appointment of Auditors
- Certificate Issued by CEO & CFO
- Subsidiary Company Transactions

- ❖ Disclosure of directorship & shareholding pattern of the company
- ❖ Responsibility of the Board in Public Subscriptions
- ❖ Roles & Responsibilities of Independent Directors
- ❖ Appointment of Stakeholders Relationship Committee
- ❖ Appointment of Nominee Directors
- ❖ Interactive Dialogue between professional bodies and corporate sector to enable evolution of corporate governance codes
- ❖ Appointment of Regulators to monitor the end use of funds collected from the public
- ❖ Credit Rating Mechanism should be followed by corporate
- ❖ Whistle-blower concept

(Irani Committee Report on Company Law (2005))

It is important to mention here that despite various recommendations made by the above committees on corporate governance, the Committees kept silence on two major issues on corporate governance. They are:

- ❖ Chairman and CEO Duality (particularly in regard to separation of these two posts), and
- ❖ Appointment of Nomination Committee.

❖ Role of SEBI

With the abolition of the office of the Controller of Capital Issues, The Security and Exchange Board of India (SEBI) was constituted. It was established originally in 1988 but was only given statutory power with enactment of the SEBI Act in January 1992. The SEBI did not obtain complete autonomy and authority to pursue its twin goals of investor protection and market development. The authority in key areas remained with the Department of Company Affairs (DCA). The statutory and regulatory powers to SEBI have been given by the Government with the mission to move from control regime to prudential regulations.

SEBI introduced a new clause 49 in the listing agreement of the stock exchanges vide its circular (SM/DRP/Policy/CIR-10/2000) dated 21st February, 2000, specifying the principles of corporate governance. Thereafter it issued circulars on 9th march, 2000, 12th September, 2000, 22nd January,2001 , 16th March, 2001, and 31st December, 2001, inter alia detailing provisions of corporate governance, its applicability, reporting requirements, amendments to clause 49. Following the recommendations of Narayana Murthy committee on corporate governance SEBI , in exercise of powers conferred by Section 11(1) of the SEBI Act 1992, read with Section 10 of the SCRA Act, 1956, revised clause 49 again vide its circular (SEBI/MRD/SE/2003/26/08) dated 26th August, 2003. But this circular was deferred for implementation and finally withdrawn by SEBI due to its controversial and debatable provisions. It was replaced by new SEBI circular (SEBI/CFD/DIL/CG/1/2004/12/10) dated 29th October, 2004, after complete overhaul of clause 49 (revised clause 49), superseding all previous circulars issued by SEBI in this regard. The provisions of the revised Clause 49 must be implemented for the following entities:

- For entities seeking listing for the first time, at the time of seeking in-principle approval for such listing.
- For existing listed entities which were required to comply with Clause 49 which is being revised , i.e. those having a paid up share capital of Rs. 30 million and above or net worth of Rs. 250 million or more at any time in the history of the company, by April 1, 2005.
- The companies complying with the provisions of the existing Clause 49 at present must continue to do so till the revised

Clause 49 is complied with or till March, 31, 2005, whichever is earlier.

- For other listed entities which are not companies, but body corporates (e.g. private and public sector banks, financial institutions, insurance companies etc.) incorporated under other statues, the revised Clause 49 would apply to the extent that it does not violate their respective statues and guidelines or directives issued by the relevant regulatory authorities. The revised Clause 49 is not applicable to mutual funds.

The main requirements of the revised Clause 49 of the Listing Agreement are summarized hereunder:

- Mandatory requirements (Annexure 1 of Clause 49) includes composition of Board, Non-executive Directors' Compensation and Disclosures, code of conduct, composition of Audit committee, meetings, role, powers of Audit committee, related party transaction, CEO/CFO certification or Compliance etc.
- Non-mandatory requirements (Annexure 1 D of Clause 49) includes Maintenance of Board, composition of remuneration committee, shareholders rights, Auditor qualification, Training of Board members, Mechanism for evaluating non-executive Board Members or Whistle Blower Policy etc.

Recently, SEBI has added some new provisions in the Clause 49 of the Listing Agreement which stipulate that:

- If the non-executive chairman of a listed company is a promoter or is related to the promoters or persons occupying management positions at the board level or one level below the board, at least one-half of the board of the company should consist of independent directors.
- An independent director should have a minimum age of 21 years.

- The time gap between the exit and entry of independent directors shall not exceed 180 days.
- The disclosures of relationships between directors shall be made in documents and filing.

Comparative Study between Clause 49 of the Listing Agreement & Sarbanes Oxley Act, 2002

The Sarbanes Oxley Act, which was signed by the US President George W. Bush into law in July 2002, has brought about sweeping changes in financial reporting. This is perceived to be the most significant change to federal securities law since 1930s. Besides directors and auditors, the act has also led down new accountability standards for security analyst and legal counsels.

In India, the CII took the lead in framing a desirable code of corporate governance in April 1998. This was followed by the recommendations of the Kumar Mangalam Birla Committee on corporate governance. This committee was appointed by SEBI. The recommendations were accepted by SEBI in December 1999 and now enshrined in Clause 49 of the listing agreement of every Indian Stock Exchange. Some of the major differences between Clause 49 & Sarbanes Oxley Act, 2002 are as follows:

- **Internal control:**

Clause 49(revised)

CEO/CFO accept responsibility for establishing and maintaining internal controls and that they have evaluated the effectiveness of the internal control systems of the company and they have disclosed to the auditors and the Audit committee, deficiencies in the design or operation of internal controls, if any, of which they are aware and the steps they have taken or propose to take to rectify these deficiencies. The role of audit committee is to review this internal control report.

Sec. 302 of Sarbanes-Oxley

The principle executive officer or officers and the principle financial officer or officers or persons performing similar functions have the responsibility of designing, establishing and maintaining the internal controls. Here in the Sarbanes Oxley Act the public company accounting oversight board will review the same and not the audit committee.

In Clause 49 the audit committee will review the internal control mechanism whereas as per the Sarbanes Oxley Act the public company accounting oversight board will review the same. In Clause 49 Internal Control is only specified but no elaborative details are given about it whereas in Sec. 404 of the Sarbanes Oxley act the details regarding the same are specified.

❖ **Audit Committee composition:**

Clause 49 (revised)

1. The audit committee shall have minimum three directors as members.
2. Two-thirds of the members of audit committee shall be independent directors.
3. All members of audit committee shall be financially literate and at least one member shall have accounting or related financial management expertise. In Sarbanes Oxley act the number of directors constituting the audit committee is not specified. Also the frequency, the time gap between the meetings of audit committee is not specified. These points are clear in the Clause 49.

Section 301 of Sarbanes-Oxley

The committee (or equivalent body) is established by the board of directors of the issuer for the purpose of overseeing the accounting and financial reporting processes of the issuer. If there is no such committee then the entire board of directors is considered to be the member of the audit committee. Each member of the company's audit committee must be a director and must otherwise be independent.

❖ **Independent Director:**

As per Clause 49 (revised)

For the purpose of the sub-clause (ii), the expression 'independent director' shall mean a non-executive director of the company who apart from receiving director's remuneration, does not have any material pecuniary relationships or transactions with the company, its promoters, its directors, its senior management or its holding company, its subsidiaries and associates which may affect independence of the director. He is not related to promoters or persons occupying management positions at the board level or at one level below the board. He has not been an executive of the company in the immediately preceding three financial years. He is not a partner or an executive or was not partner or an executive during the preceding three years, of any of the following:

- ❖ The statutory audit firm or the internal audit firm that is associated with the company.
- ❖ The legal firm(s) and consulting firm(s) that have a material association with the company.

He is not a material supplier, service provider or customer or a lessor or lessee of the company, which may affect independence of the director. He is not a substantial shareholder of the company i.e. owning two percent or more of the block of voting shares. As per the clause 49 the definition of the independent director is wider in scope than the one in Sarbanes Oxley Act.

As per Sarbanes-Oxley

In order to be considered independent the one who does not

1. Accept any consulting, advisory or other compensatory fee from the issuer.

2. Be an affiliated person of the issuer or any subsidiary thereof.

❖ **Shareholders / Investors complaints**: Clause 49 (revised)

Shareholders section in the disclosures of clause 49 states that a board committee under the chairmanship of a non-executive director shall specifically look into the redressal of shareholder and investors complaints like transfer of shares, non-receipt of balance sheet, non-receipt of declared dividends etc. This Committee shall be designated as 'Shareholders/Investors Grievance Committee'.

Sarbanes Oxley act mainly considers the accounts related queries whereas Clause 49 covers the topic in the broad sense.

Sec. 301 of Sarbanes-Oxley

As per this section, each audit committee shall establish procedures for

1. the receipt, retention and treatment of complaints received by the issuer regarding accounting, internal accounting controls or auditing matters and
2. the confidential, anonymous submission by employee of the issuer of concerns regarding questionable accounting or auditing matters.

❖ **Penal Provisions:**

Clause 49 (revised)

For violation of the listing agreement, Section 23E of Securities Contract Regulation Act, 1956 provides for a pecuniary penalty of up to Rs.25 crores on the company.

Sec. 302 of Sarbanes-Oxley

For violation of Sarbanes-Oxley Act, Section 906 imposes fines and imprisonment of up to $ 1 million and 10 years for knowing violations of Section

906, and up to $5 million and 20 years for willful violations.

- **Code of Conduct/Ethics:**

Clause 49(Revised)

The Board shall lay down a code of conduct for all Board members and senior management of the company. The code of conduct shall be posted on the website of the company. All Board members and senior management personnel shall affirm compliance with the code on an annual basis. The Annual Report of the company shall contain a declaration to this effect signed by the CEO. For this purpose, the term "senior management" shall mean personnel of the company who are members of its core management team excluding Board of Directors. Normally, this would comprise all members of management one level below the executive directors, including all functional heads.

As per the above paragraph, in the Indian context, it will be obligatory for the board of the company to lay down a code of conduct for the board members and the senior management of the company.

Section 406 of Sarbanes-Oxley

The act directs the companies to disclose if they have adopted code of conduct, if not, reasons thereof. Issuers shall adopt a code of ethics for senior financial officers, applicable to its principal financial officer and comptroller or principal accounting officer, or persons performing similar functions.

As per Sarbanes-Oxley, it restricts the code of conduct to be applicable to only 'principal financial officer and comptroller or principal accounting officer, or persons performing similar functions

- **Public Company Accounting Oversight Board (PCAOB)**

As per the Sarbanes Oxley act, a Public Company Accounting Oversight Board has been set up to oversee the audit of listed companies in order to protect investors' and public interest in matters relating to the preparation of audited financial statements.

There is no such provision in the Clause 49. In India the ICAI is legally empowered to carry out most of the regulatory, oversight and disciplinary functions outlined in the SOX Act (barring prosecution and levying of penalties). But the public perception is that the ICAI mechanisms are slow and the institute is not interested in adequately disciplining the members. In India the functions of PCAOB are carried out by various regulatory agencies viz. SEBI, RBI, ICAI, ICSI, ICWAI etc. If there were to be an Indian version of the PCAOB, then such powers would need to be withdrawn from the existing regulatory agencies and concentrated in the proposed public oversight board.

As per the Sarbanes Oxley act, a Public Company Accounting Oversight Board has been set up to oversee the audit of listed companies in order to protect investors' and public interest in matters relating to the preparation of audited financial statements.

❖ **Amendments to the Companies Act, 1956**

India took up its economic reforms programme in 1990s. Again a need was felt for a comprehensive review of the Companies Act, 1956 which has become the bulkiest and archaic with 781 sections and 25 schedules by this time. Three unsuccessful attempts were made in 1993, 1997 and then in 2003 to rewrite the company law. Companies (Amendment) Bill, 2003 which contained several important provisions relating to corporate governance was withdrawn by the Government in anticipation of another comprehensive review of the law.

As many as 24 amendments to this Act were made since 1956, of which the amendments pertaining to corporate governance and corporate sector development through the Companies (Amendments) Act, 1999, the Companies (Amendment) Act, 2000 and the Companies (Amendment) Act, 2001.

The important amendments having overall implications for corporate governance are listed below:

- **The Companies (Amendment) Act, 1999**
    - Buy back of shares (Section 77A)
    - Issue of sweat equity shares (Section 79A)
    - Establishment of investor education and protection fund (Section 205(c))
    - Liberalization of Inter-corporate loans and investment norms.
- **The Companies (amendment) Act, 2000**

Penalties increased by almost ten times for non-compliance in various Sections of the Act

- Issue of shares with differential rights (Section 86)
- Passing of resolutions by postal ballot (Section 192A)
- Directors' Responsibility Statement (Section 217(2AA))
- Additional powers and duties of auditors (Section 227)
- Minimum number of directors including election of small shareholders' director (Section 252)
- Maximum number of directorships in companies reduced from 20 to 15 (Section 275)
- Audit Committee (Section 292A)

- **The Companies (amendment) Act, 2009**

Some of the amendments to the companies Act which are remarkable and have a direct bearing on improvement in the standards of corporate governance are explained below:

- Passing of resolution by Postal Ballot (section 192A)
- Instead of transacting the business in the general meeting, public listed company, resolutions relating to such business as the central government may, by notification, declare to be conducted only by Postal Ballot.
- The company when decides to pass resolution by postal ballot, it shall send a notice to all shareholders by registered post.

- If a resolution requires requisites majority of the shareholders by means of postal ballot, it shall be deemed to have been duly passed at a general meeting convened in that behalf.
- Under Directors' Responsibility Statement (217(2AA)) section, the board's report shall include a 'Directors' Responsibility Statement'.

Chapter 4

DEVELOPMENTS IN CORPORATE GOVERNANCE AREA

"Corporate Governance is philosophy which touches every facet of the functioning of a Corporate and its stakeholders. It is not an end in itself but a means to practice and bring about corporate democracy at all levels of the corporate entity."

– ***Harsh Mariwala, Chairman & Managing Director,***

– ***Marico Industries Ltd.***

The fundamentals of Corporate Governance have its deep roots in Indian history. But surprisingly it is very less known to us. Our own ancient texts have laid down sound principles of governance which seem very relevant to modern day corporate requirements.

The Governor and Committee Men submitted frequent reports on their more important decisions for confirmation of meetings or 'General Courts' of all subscribers of the Company, corresponding to the general meetings of company shareholders in the present day. (European Settlements, C S Srinivasachari, in The History and Culture of the Indian People, Volume 7, The Mughal Empire, (1994), endnote 5 to chapter XVI, (p.518), Bharatiya Vidya Bhavan)

In this context, it would be appropriate to recall the Kautilyan admonition to his King, "In the happiness of his subject lies the King's happiness; in their welfare his welfare." (The Arthashastra, kautilya

(Ca.4th Century B.C), English Transection by L N Rangarajan, (1992), Penguin Books.)

The main key three authorities for the survey of similarities between the Governance Structures of the ancient Kingdom and the Modern Governance are:

1. Rig Veda
2. The Dharam Shastras
3. Mahabharatha

The Mahabharata offers several other inputs into the ideal conduct and characteristics of a king all of which could be suitably adapted to the modern corporate chief executive. Standing out far and ahead of the detailed listing of these attributes is the concern the King should have for his subjects and the respect and heed that he should extend to his counselors, who should of course themselves, be beyond blemish. Reviewing these edicts, one can easily comprehend the close similarities between the governance structures of the ancient kingdoms and modern corporations.

- **Role of Corporate Boards as Advisors and Monitors of Management**

The Monitoring role of the board of directors has been the subject of extensive empirical research. Both the Business Roundtable and the American Law Institute (Monks and Minnow 1996, p. 172) list advising management among the top five functions of the board of directors in the United States.

The Advisory role of the board exists not only in the United States but also in Europe where boards in several countries are formally separated into a Management board and a Supervisory board.

The Monitoring role of the board has been studied extensively in a large, mostly empirical literature but the advisory role has received little attention. At first glance the advisory and monitoring roles of a sole board complement each other, because the board can use the information the manager provides both to make better recommendations and better evaluations.

Hermalin and Weisbach (1998) documents that the relationship between board composition and CEO career concerns may be influenced by succession issues. They provide evidence that firms add insiders to the board when CEOs are near retirement. This suggests that the relation between monitoring and career concerns is difficult to interpret when monitoring is proxied by board composition.

❖ **Corporations and its Shareholders**

The Shareholders contribute some of their money to the equity capital of the Corporation. They are presumed to bear a greater portion of the risks of running a firm and hence expected to be rewarded for this risk. They are supposed to own the corporation. But only the left-over earning belong to the shareholders. In this sense, they bear the largest risk with their wealth and it is the duty and obligation of the managers, who are the agents of the shareholders, to maximize this wealth.

However, Sumantra Ghoshal argues that this principle, along with the agency theory, has lead to a gross over-emphasis on shareholders' value. Shareholders, unlike most other stakeholders, have the *earliest* exit option and hence carry the *least* risk with a firm. Much of the corporate governance theories still use the agency theory as their kingpin and have failed to gather any evidence on their effectiveness even in improving the shareholder value. (Ghoshal Sumantra (2005)).

❖ **Board and Directors Legal Dimensions**

The Cadbury Report (1992) described the board responsibility in more succinctly phraseology, to include setting the company's strategies aims, providing the leadership to put them into effect, supervising the management of the business, and reporting to shareholders on their stewardship. More recently, the Commonwealth

Association for Corporate Governance articulated the role and responsibilities of the board in greater details. Some of such principles are as follow:

- ❖ Ensure that through a managed and effective process board appointments are made that provide a mix of proficient directors, each of whom is able to add value and to bring independent judgment to bear on the decision-making process.
- ❖ Ensure that the corporation complies with all relevant laws, regulations, and codes of best business practice.

In India, the SEBI (Kumar Mangalam Birla) Report [Report of the committee appointed by the SEBI on Corporate Governance under the Chairmanship of Shri Kumar Managalam Birla, January, 2000.] on Corporate Governance (KMB) describes this role as providing leadership and strategic guidance, objective and independent judgment, and control over the company in the discharge of its accountability to the shareholders.

The Company's (Amendment) Bill, 2003, however seeks to prescribe that public companies with a minimum paid up capital and free reserves of Rs.50.00 million or a turnover of Rs.500 million should have a minimum of seven Directors. No public company may have more than 15 directors on its board. Neither the CII Code [Desirable Corporate Governance- A Code, (1998), Confederation of Indian Industry.) nor the KMB Report (2000) had any such stipulations on this point. A minimum number of 7 directors have been recommended by the Naresh Chandra Committee on Corporate Audit and Governance, 2003, Department of Company Affairs, Government of India.

A quick survey of thirty companies listed in the Bombay Stock Exchange, provides with some interesting data. A broad-size survey of a large sample of 285 companies brought out the following interesting statistics. (www.bseindia.com):

- The average and medium size is 9, which has been quite stable during the years covered.
- Maximum board size has ranged from 17 to 19, with 18 being most common.
- Most companies in the sample for most number of years considered fall in the range of 9 to 11 Directors.
- From 2000 onwards, the trend seems to signal a downward movement towards the size of 6 to 8.

However, what is perhaps more important than size is the composition of the board of directors in terms of their ability to discharge their responsibilities in the interest of all the shareholders, especially in the context of separation and distancing between ownership and control.

The (Ganguly) Committee Report of the Consultative Group of Directors of Banks / Financial Institutions, 2002, Reserve Bank of India has recommended that it would be desirable to separate the office of Chairman and Managing Director in respect of large public sector banks. (The (Ganguly) Committee Report of the Consultative Group of Directors of Banks / Financial Institutions, 2002, Reserve Bank of India.)

- **Controlling Shareholders and Corporate Governance**

Public Companies in the world except United States and United Kingdom typically have a single shareholder or group of shareholders with effective voting control, often but not invariably without corresponding equity holdings. In nine East Asian Countries, Professor Stijn Claessens, Simeon Djankov, and Larry H.P Lang found a single shareholder control in more than two thirds of listed companies. (Claessens, Djankov & Lang, Supra note 7, at 92 table 3, 93-94)

The appropriate distinction is between the widely held and controlling shareholding system that supports diversity of shareholder distribution and system that essentially support controlling shareholder distribution. The research work done earlier by Ronald J.

Gilson on controlling shareholder regimes has taken two general decisions:

- ❖ The First direction reflected in series of articles by Rafael La Porta, Florencio Lopez-de-Silanes, Andrei Shleifer, and Robert Vishny, linked the breadth of shareholder distribution to the quality of Jurisdictions' Law. In this account, controlling shareholder regimes exist in jurisdiction whose legal systems do not protect minority shareholders from dominant shareholders' diversion of private benefits of control. *(See sources cited infra note 20 pg. 1644 of IIMB Sessions, 2007)*
- ❖ The Second direction finds the explanation for concentrated ownership patterns in politics. In an important book, Prof. Mark Roe identified social democratic politics as the driving force towards ownership concentration. [Mark J. Roe, Political Determinants of corporate governance: political context, corporate impact 2003].

It is also commonplace in Europe for control by a dominant shareholder to result from structural devices that leverage voting rights above the level of equity investment. E.g. Data produced below regarding Use of Dual Class Stock to leverage Voting Rights shows that these many percentages of listed companies in respective countries issue dual class of common stock, with one class having dramatically higher voting rights.

❖ Control & Conflicts

A more sincere responsibility of corporate boards is to develop mechanisms to identify and appropriately steer clear of potential or actual situation of conflict in the context of the company's business operations. Such conflict situations arise fundamentally from the boards' and individual directors' fiduciary duties or obligations to their company and its shareholders. Directors owe their obligation for fair dealing to their company and its shareholders. This calls for appropriate and comprehensive disclosure of interest involved, leaving it to the other disinterested directors to decide whether the transaction should still be put to through because of its possible overall benefit to the corporation. In all such disclosures, two dimensions of disclosures need to be considered: one relating to the conflict of interest per se, and the other to the material facts of the transaction.

Another critical principle in the field of conflict of interest situations is that directors may not advance their pecuniary interest by engaging in competition with the corporation, without the disinterested directors on the board authorizing (or ratifying) such action in the larger interest of the company, or approved by disinterested shareholders, such approval not being equivalent to a waste of the company's assets. Some examples from recent Indian experience are here below enumerated, to highlight the practical implications of potential conflict of interest situations that boards and directors have to address from time to time. Board Vs. Dominant Shareholders:

1. Differences over business strategies to be followed.
2. Differences over Ownership and Control.
3. Board Vs. Ownership issues.
4. Board Vs. Individual Directors.

❖ **Audit Committees**

Audit Committees have been mandated since June 1978 for all the companies listed on the New York Stock Exchange. These committees were to be constituted "solely of directors independent of management and free from any relationship that, in the opinion of the Board of Directors, would interfere with the exercise of independent judgment as a committee member. Over a period of time all the other stock exchanges in the United States have fallen in line and require their listed companies to have such Audit Committees.

Canada, Australia, Israel, Malaysia, Hong Kong, and (more recently) India all mandate an Audit Committee of the board in law in respect of all listed and / or other public limited companies. A recent survey revealed that 85% of the companies studied reported having an Audit Committee, and 55% of the sample confirmed their Audit Committees comprised solely of Independent directors. [Egon Zehnder Board of Directors Global Study 2000, (2001), Egon Zehnder International].

Following the Narayana Murthy Committee Report (2004), the SEBI mandated amendment to Clause 49 of the Listing Agreement prescribes that "all members of the Audit Committee shall be non-executive directors, with the majority of members and its chairman being independent directors, and at least one of them having accounting or related financial management experience."

The KMB Report and the Listing Agreement as amended by the January 2006 clause 49 prescribe that no director shall be a member of more than ten committees or be the chairperson of more than five committees across all companies where he or she is a director.

Thus, from the research study held by different countries, researcher can make out that Audit Committee and other Committees of Board of Directors have also been given due importance in Corporate Governance.

❖ **Bank Governance**

A scam of severe magnitude comparable to a scaled-down version of the Black- Monday disaster of September 1987 on the New York Stock Exchange and other related markets, shocked Indian Stock markets in 1992-93; later in that decade itself, The Indian Government had to mount a bail-out operation to protect the State Controlled Unit Trust of India. Numerous non-banking financial companies came to grief during this period; 2001 also saw some of cooperative banks being afflicted and moving towards liquidation. (Dr. N Balasubramanain (2007)

The Basel Committee on bank supervision has published numerous papers on specific topics of interest and relevance to banks.

It is important that these together with the guidance received from the Reserve Bank of India are part of the training and education curriculum at Banks' staff training colleges, so that not only what needs to be done and how but also the why of it all can be understood and appreciated by executive managements in banks at different operating levels.

There are essentially two prongs to the banks' role in promoting good governance; first they should set an example, in terms of laying down good governance procedures, and even more importantly, internalizing such processes; and second, they can do a world of good by insisting that their customers who borrow from them follow similar good-governance regimes in their businesses.

❖ **Public Sector Governance**

Governance of State Owned Enterprises (SOE) is important from two significant perspectives: to demonstrate that first, the government as the controlling owner, was following principles and practices of good governance, and second, more importantly, the government was setting an example to the other corporations in the private, joint, and the cooperative sectors, on the actual practice of good governance.

"The state and the SOE should recognize the rights of all shareholders and in accordance with the OECD principles of Corporate Governance ensure their equitable treatment and equal access to corporate information."

(Dr. N Balasubramanian (2007))

Some of the most common issues that surface in this connection are

- ❖ Unfair transfer of Corporate Resources to other, "related" entities or even individual, and Right to vote on appointment of auditors, on approval of audited accounts of the company, and as noted earlier, on appointments to the board of directors etc.

- Does Corporate Governance ensure transparency, full disclosures & accountability of companies to all its stakeholders? – Summary of FICCI & GT survey 2009

This question's answer is given in recent survey conducted by FICCI & Grant Thornton. (CG Review 2009: India 101-500 A review of corporate governance practices at the mid market listed companies in India by FICCI & GT.) The FICCI GT: India 101-500 CGR 2009 was designed to analyze corporate governance practices at 'mid-market' listed companies in India. The review methodology was based on a survey to gauge the nature and extent of corporate governance practices and approximately 400 companies across various sectors were targeted to participate in the survey except top 100 companies in India.

FICCI & Grant Thornton review uncovers that corporate India sees significant value in the adoption of the prescribed corporate governance practices, with 84% of the respondents stating that compliance with Clause 49 enhances the perceptions of their stakeholders on the conduct of the company's business. This is possibly also an indication of the mindset of Indian companies where stakeholders' perception is considered as an extremely important business driver.

To the extent that such considerations result in decisions that seek to enhance shareholder value, is a positive sign. An overwhelming majority of the respondents (68%) felt that Clause 49 was adequate to bring requisite levels of transparency in their business and a even larger proportion saw the benefits extending to improved processes and controls (84%), enhanced awareness of roles (74%) and better risk management (74%) in their companies.

While a relatively small proportion (9%) of the respondents were in the process of developing a suitable strategy to comply with Clause 49, approximately one third of the respondents (32%) believed that they did not need independent assurance on various initiatives undertaken by them internally, to achieve the desired levels of compliance. Possibly, this is also a reflection of a relatively cautious and "wait and see" approach that such companies would typically adopt to new regulations.

A majority of the respondents (53%) had supplemented such internal initiatives with external help on specific aspects such as those relating to assessment of controls, enterprise wide risk management, and institutionalization of a compliance framework and implementation of a code of conduct. An overwhelming majority of the respondents (61%) felt that compliance norms should differ and should be based on company size; and this will result in achieving the desired levels of governance in spirit rather than the letter of the law. This is possibly the strongest signal to the lawmakers that a "one size fits all" approach may not necessary yield the desired levels of compliance in India.

A majority of the respondents (56%) felt that an ideal board structure should have between 25% and 50% as independent directors. What appears to have come out strongly is that the bane of the issue relating to the availability of independent directors is in the process adopted by companies to appoint independent directors. A majority of the respondents (56%) disclosed that they did not have a nomination committee to lead the process of appointing independent directors in their companies.

While 66% of the respondents also felt the need for the development of a predetermined charter with specific KRAs for the members of the board and audit committees, 37% felt that their companies could do more in terms of a formal and tailored induction program for their new directors.

All respondents claimed that their board was meeting at least once every quarter and at regular intervals in accordance with the provisions of section 285 of the Companies Act. A large number (48%) disclosed that their board was meeting between 6 to 8 times in a year.

From the above study, the researcher can surely say like those corporate governance codes (clause 49) fulfill the requirements of disclosure, transparency and accountability of various stakeholders. However, it still remains in the hands of the corporate bodies to fulfill these requirements or not.

❖ **Selected Key Governance Parameters**

Prof. Das in his research "Corporate Governance in India- an evaluation", has taken 40 select companies for the FY 2004-05 to show the quality of corporate governance practiced in the sampled companies. He has developed his model for measurement of corporate governance, wherein certain parameters have been highlighted and weight age has been assigned to each such parameter. Some of the key parameters are Structure & Strength of the Board, Appointment of Lead Independent Director, Board Committees, Disclosure of Remuneration Policy & Remuneration of Directors, Disclosures & Transparency and Disclosure of Stakeholders' interests to name a few. These key governance parameters have been selected on a 90 point scale. He has then further ranked the companies and industry groups on a five point scale from Excellent to Poor.

On analyzing, Prof. Das has put forward his findings. His results of evaluation on corporate governance standards adopted and practiced by the select companies as disclosed in their annual reports have been graded as Excellent to Poor. Rank 1 has been awarded to Infosys (Excellent). The "Very Good" grade was lead by Dabur India, the "Good" grade, which consisted of the majority of the select companies was lead by Dr. Reddy's Laboratories, whereas the "Average" grade was tailed by Zee Telefilms. Overall, Prof. Das has found out that among his 48 selected companies, only 1 scored Excellent, 6 scored Very Good, 35 scored Good and 6 companies scored Average.

He did not find any of the select companies to be in the "Poor" grade. (Subhash Chandra Das (2009))

- **Some Important Overview of Experts**

Mckinsey's survey (Fernando 2010) of Corporate Governance conducted a survey with a sample size of 188 companies from 6 emerging markets (including India) to determine the correlation between good corporate governance and the market valuation of the company. The results of the survey pointed out to a positive correlation between the two. The researcher too has developed a corporate governance index which determines the correlation between corporate governance with the profitability of the company, (specifically the net profit ratio).

The FICCI & Grant Thornton survey of 2009, covering approximately 400 companies across various sectors, points out that Corporate Governance ensures transparency, full disclosures and accountability of companies to all its stakeholders. FICCI & Grant Thornton review uncovers that corporate India sees significant value in the adoption of the prescribed corporate governance practices. This is possibly also an indication of the mindset of Indian companies where stakeholders' perception is considered as an extremely important business driver. In the line of the above study, the researcher can surely say that these corporate governance codes (clause 49) fulfill the requirements of disclosure, transparency and accountability of various stakeholders. (In the context of page number 69-71 of the thesis). However, it still remains in the hands of the corporate bodies to fulfill or not to fulfill these requirements, hence the researcher has undertaken the task to analyze the parameters of Transparency & disclosures, CG & Auditors' certificate, Structure & strength, Board Independence & Chairperson, Appointment of Independent Directors – Board Committees, Stakeholder Value Enhancement, Effectiveness of BOD, Board Systems & Procedure, Board

Committees – Audit Committee, Board Committees – Shareholder Grievance, CSR, etc.

Prof. Das in his research "Corporate Governance in India - an evaluation" has taken 40 select companies for the FY 2004-05 to show the quality of corporate governance practiced in the sampled companies, and have graded them in a score of 90. Whereas this researcher goes a step beyond by taking a sample of 50 select companies from a combination of four different sectors and BSE 30 Group companies as secondary data, and has graded them in a score of 100, through various corporate governance parameters. The researcher has then constructed a corporate governance index covering 12 parameters and has assigned a score on the basis of primary data collected from Company secretaries' responses to question number 27, thereby giving more depth and clarity to the issue. (In the context of page number 80-81 of the thesis)

The investigations of Beverley Jackling and Shireenjit Johl (Jackling & Johl, 2009) established the relationship between internal governance structures and financial performance of Indian companies. The effectiveness of boards of directors, including board composition, board size, and aspects of board leadership including duality and board busyness are addressed in the Indian context. The study used a sample of top Indian companies taking into account the endogeneity of the relationships among corporate governance, corporate performance, and corporate capital structure. The initial sample for this study comprises a sample from the top Indian companies listed on the Bombay Stock Exchange (BSE) by market capitalization in the year ended March 31, 2006. As of March 31, 2006 (Annual Report 2005-06), all companies in the sample considered for this study were required to comply with the revised Clause 49 listing requirements. The study provides some support for aspects of agency theory as a greater proportion of independent directors on boards were associated with improved firm performance. The findings suggest that larger board size has a positive impact on performance.

The study however failed to support terms of the association between frequency of board meetings and performance. However, the nature of business structures in India, for example the large number of family businesses, may limit the generalizability of the findings and signals the need for further investigation of these businesses.

In order to study the various aspects of good corporate governance, the researcher has taken into considerations factors like board independence, board committees, CEO and Chairperson's duality, Board systems and procedures (frequency of board meetings) etc.

Chapter 5

OUTLOOK OF CORPORATE GOVERNANCE

"Corporate governance is vital in medium and long-term perspective to enable companies to compete globally in a sustained manner and make them flourish and grow. Corporate Governance is not merely about enacting legislation but about establishing a climate of trust and confidence among various constituents. In a dynamic corporate environment, it is acknowledged by all concerned that good and effective Corporate Governance is very important for an efficient and vibrant capital and financial market."

– Yogendra Kr. Modi, Former President, FICCI.

Recent events in India have put the spotlight on corporate governance practices of Indian Companies. A key aspect that is being debated in the corridors of Indian corporate is whether the country needs major regulatory changes to improve corporate governance, or whether improved standards of corporate governance could be achieved through adoption of principle-based standards of conduct. India Inc. has generally been proactive in promulgating corporate governance regulations. In doing so, a good balance has been achieved i.e. headway has been made, in terms of helping ensure that regulations are not stifling country's entrepreneurial initiatives. From a purely regulatory standpoint, India compares favorably with most other developing and Asian Economics as far as its corporate governance rules are concerned.

As noted earlier, good corporate governance is managed through various authorities such as Board of Directors, various mandatory and non-mandatory board committees, statutory auditor and compliance officer. A diligent role is played by the compliance officer, who normally is a company secretary or a statutory auditor.

The company secretary has the responsibility of directly liaisoning with the investors and regulatory authorities such as SEBI, Stock Exchanges, Registrar of Companies (ROC), RBI, DCA etc. in respect of implementation of various laws, rules, regulations and other directives of such authorities and also in respect of investor service and complaints.

Further, the company secretary should act as Compliance Officer in respect of complaints received and should effectively monitor the share transfer and other related processes and report to the Company's Board in each meeting about the same. It is a good practice to inform the Board, reasons for delay in redressing shareholders' /investors' complaints. This is usually done by the company secretary.

The Company Secretary's or Statutory Auditor's Certificate on compliance of condition of Corporate Governance as prescribed by the Clause 49 of Listing Agreement, must be attached as an Annexure to the Director's Report made under section 217 of the Companies Act, 1956. A copy of the certificate must also be sent to the concerned stock exchange(s) along with the Annual Return filed by the company. Compliance Certificate must be obtained before the date of the Board meeting at which the Board's Report according to section 217 of the Companies Act, 1956 will be placed for Board's approval.

Due to the utmost importance of the Company Secretary, in the well being of good governance, the researcher conducted a survey on corporate governance views by the means of a questionnaire across 100 company secretaries.

This survey, conducted between January 2010 & February 2010, involved over 100 respondents comprising practicing & full time employed company secretaries, belonging to the city of Ahmedabad, who were asked about their opinion, experience and the outlook for corporate governance in India.

Some aspects covered in this survey include:

- Corporate Governance Regulations in India
- Corporate Governance Concerns in India and role of Independent Directors and Audit Committees addressing these concerns
- Board Practices, Board oversight of Risk Management and the importance of given to integrity and ethical values.
- Practices those are fundamental towards improved corporate governance.
- Corporate Governance Standards enforced through regulations or principle based.
- Role of different entities in improving corporate governance.
- Role of Industries in fulfillment of corporate governance compliances and voluntary disclosures.
- Framing of Corporate Governance Index.

- **Legal aspects of Corporate Governance**

Clause 49 should not be considered as the only legal aspect of Corporate Governance, but the new companies Act, accounting standards, Secretarial standards also play an important role in shaping Corporate Governance. Yet as a general practice, Clause 49 is considered as the ultimate litmus test for a good Corporate Governance. Here six important views are taken into consideration. They range from the impact of Clause 49, the redressal for changes, to the impact of Company act.

Introduction of Clause 49 Change in corporate governance levels in India after introduction of Clause 49

Options	No. of Responses	% of Responses
No Significant Change	8	8
Significant improvement opportunity exists	60	60
There has been a marked improvement	32	32
Total	100	100

An overall view suggests that though there is a significant change, there still exists opportunities for improvement. After the introduction of clause 49, one third of the respondents are of the opinion that there is a good improvement in the corporate governance of the corporate. While most of the remaining respondents think that changes have occurred, but clause 49 has the potential of bringing in radical changes, with the intervention of SEBI.

Strength of Clause 49 Strength of Clause 49 to inculcate good governance practices

Options	No. of Responses	% of Responses
Existing Clause 49 is sufficient	25	25
Clause 49 requires only a few changes	51	51
Clause 49 can be revamped significantly	24	24
Total	100	100

Looking at the study, half of the respondents feel and believe that Clause 49 is strong enough and if a few changes are inculcated in the clause, it can lead to good governance practices. Where as one fourth was of the opinion that the existing clause is sufficient enough, and an equal number believed that there was a dire need of revamping Clause 49.

Half of the respondents were of the opinion that the penalty levels were not sufficient in India to discipline poor and unethical governance practice. Though, this should not deter one from understanding the reason behind it. Yet, an equal number of respondents felt that there was no impact of such penalty levels, and the same number did not even know what difference such levels made. Only

14% of the questioned company secretaries stated that the existing penalty levels are sufficient to put good governance in place.

❖ **Corporate Governance Concerns**

A major concern for Corporate Governance is the reasons for failure of corporate in India and the west. Many views were handled by the researcher as regards to the primary concerns, and those which, if existing, could be overcome with minor changes. Some of them are the issues related to the role played by independent director, issues of minority share holders, timely packaged and readily available information for discharging of board duties, sustainability of the company related to responsiveness of board of directors and the debate of stock options.

Risks to corporate governance in India

Biggest risks to corporate governance in India

Options	No. of Responses	% of Responses
Low Financial discipline	17	11
Lack of respect for shareholder community	38	26
Weak oversight and monitoring mechanisms	42	28
Inadequate independence	24	16
Management override	28	19
Total	149	100

To the query as to which were the biggest risks to corporate governance in India, a majority of 28% respondents said that it was due to weak oversight and monitoring mechanisms, whereas 26% were of the opinion that it was due to lack of respect for shareholder community. 19% felt that it was due to management override, and 16% said that it was due to inadequate independence. Only a meager 11% were of the opinion that it was due to low financial discipline.

Reasons for the corporate failures in the West

Biggest reasons for the corporate failures in the West

Options	No. of Responses	% of Responses
Low Financial discipline	29	22
Lack of respect for shareholder community	19	14
Weak oversight and monitoring mechanisms	48	36
Inadequate independence	15	11
Management override	21	16
Total	132	100

An interesting fact came out, when the respondents were asked as to what were the biggest reasons for the corporate failures in the West. A good 36% were of the opinion that it was due to weak oversight and monitoring mechanisms, and 22% of the respondents felt that low financial discipline was the main reason. 16% gave Management override as their response, and 14% gave lack of respect for shareholder community as their option. Only a 11% felt that inadequate independence could be the biggest reasons for the corporate failures in the West.

❖ **Corporate Governance by Indian companies**

Many aspects are related to Corporate Governance practices by Indian companies were studied. Of them, risk management practices were given prominence. Also the view of the quality of Management Discussion and Analysis report of Companies was studied. Effectiveness of board committees and skill sets of the Audit committees were looked upon. Here again the researcher emphasized upon the importance of various committees.

Current standards of risk management practices in Indian Companies

Rating for current standards of risk management practices in Indian Companies

Options	No. of Responses	% of Responses
High	3	3
Medium	52	52
Needs Improvement	45	45
Total	100	100

Over half the respondents felt that the rating for current standards of risk management practices in Indian Companies was quite medium. Just a shade below half the respondents were of the opinion that the rating for current standards of risk management practices in Indian Companies needs improvement. Only 3 of the respondents said that the rating for current standards of risk management practices in Indian Companies was high enough.

Quality of Management Discussion and Analysis report of Companies

Quality of Management Discussion and Analysis Report of Companies

Options	No. of Responses	% of Responses
Low	21	21
Moderate	65	65
High	14	14
Total	100	100

65% respondents rated the quality of Management Discussion and Analysis Report of Companies as moderate with 21% voting it as low. 14% of the respondents gave a high rating to the quality of Management Discussion and Analysis Report of Companies.

❖ **Improving and enforcing of Corporate Governance**

Various parameters were asked to be defined as important for

better Corporate Governance. The researcher also put forward certain parameters to be prioritized as more effective than the others.

Many statements related to such parameters and standards of improvement are discussed here.

Standards of Corporate Governance

How could the corporate governance be improved and enhanced upon was a challenging task for the researcher, which was thoroughly performed with accuracy and ease. 23% of the respondents felt that by considerable improvements in financial disclosure and Management Discussion and Analysis, positive changes in this field can be brought about. 20% of them felt that by significantly enhancing powers of independent directors, changes could be brought about. An equal number of 18 respondents each gave a nod to strengthening rights of minority shareholders through statute and to separation of position of chairman and CEO. 21% diligently favored the need of drastically improving risk management and oversight processes.

- **Ethics and corporate social responsibilities**

Utmost importance is emphasized on high morale for ethics and values. Responsibility towards betterment of society as general is also a fore front runner. The researcher looked upon if CSR was high on the agenda of Indian companies and if ethical values and integrity matter to Indian companies.

Corporate social responsibility

Though Corporate Social Responsibility (CSR) should be on a high scale on any good corporate governance, 42% of the respondents thought that maybe CSR is high on the agenda of Indian companies. 10% of them were undecided. 19% were found on the affirmative side and 29% were found on the negation side.

Integrity and ethical values.

Though a high number of 61% of the respondents felt that the integrity and ethical values given due importance by Indian companies, a lot could be improved upon. 26% thought that such due importance was not given. 11% felt that such importance existed and 2 respondents chose to be neutral.

- **Opinions regarding Corporate Governance practices**

A varied opinion was found regarding Corporate Governance practices. The researcher prodded upon sensitive issues such as who should monitor effectiveness of corporate governance practices at companies, and should Corporate Governance be enforced through regulations or should it be principle based. Also issues related to whose role is important for improving Corporate Governance in our country and how the Corporate Governance index would be rated upon various parameters & their rankings were studied. A detailed study on which industries, among the select sectors are best performing was also undertaken.

authority to monitor effectiveness of corporate governance practices at companies

As to whom the Authority to monitor effectiveness of corporate governance practices at companies be handed over, a whopping 69% felt that it should be via corporate governance audits through selected corporate governance specialist. Rating Agencies were prioritized at 23%. 13% gave the boards this opportunity, and 10% gave it to the public, i.e. investors / minority shareholder groups may have access to full information to monitor effectiveness of corporate governance.

Enforcement of Corporate Governance standards.

The existing (Clause 49) and ensuing (The Companies Bill, 2008) legislations to cover the fundamentals of effective corporate governance and India compares favorably with most other developing and Asian economies as far as the adequacy of corporate governance regulations are concerned.

Improved corporate governance, however, does not solely rest on control through increased regulations. What is required is a principle-based approach developed on fundamentals, preventing moral fragility that is enforced through pragmatic levels of regulations.

Enforcement or education was the question of essence. Should corporate governance standards should be enforced through regulations or principle based, was tricky in nature. Yet 72% respondents diplomatically said that principle based standards with moderate regulations and strong regulatory review mechanism should be implemented. An equal number of 14% were seen on the extreme poles of regulations and principles.

- **Reliability of the Aspects of Corporate Governance**

The reliability test (Cronbach's Alpha) is used in survey instruments to probe underlying constructs that the researcher wants to measure. These are consisting of indexed responses to the questionnaire, and then are later summed to arrive at a resultant score. The aspects taken into consideration are: legal aspects of corporate governance, corporate governance concerns, corporate governance practices by Indian companies, improving & enforcing of corporate governance, ethics & corporate social responsibility and opinions regarding corporate governance practices. These aspects further have all the questions which are included in the questionnaire which was analyzed by the researcher.

Usually, development of such scales is not the end of the research itself, but rather a means to gather predictor variables for use in objective models. The higher the score, the more reliable the generated scale is. Nunnaly (1978) has indicated 0.6 to be an acceptable reliability coefficient. The results of the reliability tests are shown in table 6.69 having an average of 0.63, which is acceptable.

The main reason to develop the hypotheses is to measure the consistency of the primary data collected. It was observed by the researcher that there was a difference in the rules (codes and laws) and practices.

For instance, auditor's certificate is mandatory for secretarial audit (rule), yet the respondents feel that there is a weak monitoring mechanism within the companies (practice). Similarly, transparency and disclosures for shareholders have maximum importance (rule), but the respondents feel that the biggest risk for corporate governance in India is lack of respect for the shareholders' community (practice). Again, the Companies Act, Listing Agreement and SEBI guidelines specifically provide for the listed companies on the conduct of the Meetings, like the time granted to perform the duties (rule). The respondents felt that the board procedures did not give sufficient time to the board to perform their duties (practice). Moreover, audit committees are mandatory (rule). But the ratings given by the respondents to the skill sets of Indian audit committee is moderate (practice). Citing the above (few) mentioned points, the researcher felt motivated to hypothesize and check the various aspects of governance if such practical differences were consistent and prevalent within all the select sectors.

A majority of the companies though making huge and remarkable profits do not necessarily practice good Corporate Governance. This is shown in the findings with the help of co-relation statistics (page number 266). Here, the researcher wants to point out that Net profit ratio may just be a silver lining, and not hold much importance in view of good corporate governance. For example, the overall number 1 ranked in good corporate governance, Wipro Ltd., has secured a half way rank in net profit ratio within its own I.T. Sector, and a rank of 18 among 50 select companies. ICICI Bank Ltd, secured rank *numero uno* in net profit ratio, but got the twelfth rank in good corporate governance. These, and various other examples, show that a majority of the companies though making huge and remarkable profits do not necessarily practice good Corporate Governance.

As a general practice, Clause 49 is considered as the ultimate litmus test for a good Corporate Governance (page number 271). The researcher has found that the New Companies Act has a positive impact on Corporate Governance and though penalty levels are low to discipline poor and unethical governance, there is a significant improvement opportunity to exist in corporate governance level in India.

There is a vast scope of improving and enforcing Corporate Governance (page number 273). On the basis of the study of company secretaries' opinions, the researcher found, that as there is less financial disclosure, less Management Discussion & Analysis; less independent boards and less transparent processes in practice than in rule; there exists scope for improvement in that area. There should be a strong internal Governance mechanism.

❖ **IT GOVERNANCE**

In many organizations, IT is fundamental to support, sustain and grow the business. W%ile many organizations recognize the potential benefits that technology can yield, the successful ones also understand and manage the risks associated with implementing new technologies (W1). The IT governance is an integral part of enterprise governance that consists of the leadership, organizational structures, processes that ensure the organization's IT sustains, and extends the organization's strategies and objectives (W1). The IT governance drives strategic alignment between IT and the business and mustjudiciously measure performance (Brown and Magill 1994). So, is an integral part of enterprise governance which operates model for how organization will make decisions about use of IT, involves external relationships for obtaining IT relationships, involves authority, control, accountability, roles, and responsibilities, involves processes and methods for making decisions and involves judgments about how well use of IT enables strategic direction (Brown and Magill, 1994).

Today businesses rely on IT as an integral part of their overall enterprise strategy. A new field of thought called IT governance has been under development for several years. Just as business management is governed by generally accepted good practices, IT should be governed by practices that help to ensure an enterprise's IT resources are used responsibly, its risks are managed appropriately and its information and related technology support business objectives (Schwarz and Hirschheim, 2003). In other words, IT governance is the process by which decisions are made around IT investments. How these decisions are made, who makes the decisions, which is held accountable, and how the results of the decisions are measured and monitored are all parts of IT governance (Luftman, 2000). While there is no 'standard' definition, in general, IT governance involves specifying the decision rights, the accountability and authority framework for important IT decisions, with the objective of encouraging 'desirable behavior' in the use of IT (ITGI, 2004).

IT governance has come to play an important role in organizations where technologies are implemented in larger scales than ever before and supports numerous business operations (Posthumusa and Solms, 2005). Organizations today work in a new era of competition that is not only faster but also more turbulent, more global and more digital, requiring inexorable cost-efficiencies as well as flexibility and creativity to find new ways to innovate and create value (Grembergen, 2003). Enterprises can use IT governance for directing and controlling the technological aspects of their organization (Posthumusa and Solms, 2005). It ensures that investments in IT will generate the values the business requires and that risks associated with IT are alleviated (Grembergen, 2003). The IT Governance Institute believes IT governance to be an integral part of the overall enterprise governance. They compare the need of IT governance integration with the overall governance to the need of IT to be an integral part of the enterprise rather than be something that is practised outside the enterprise framework (ITGI, 2003). According to the IT Governance Institute, IT governance is the responsibility of the board of directors and the executive management, and is an integral part of enterprise governance. It elevates information as a key organizational asset and treats governance of information at par with governance of other assets like human, financial, intellectual, and relationship assets (Schwarz and Hirschheim, 2003).

Chapter 6

CONCLUSION

Transparency and disclosure

Due awareness in the market, almost all the select companies scored high on the transparency and disclosure parameter. The banking sector, contrary to its clean image, is not complying at par with other sectors in the transparency and disclosure parameter. There should be unison in guidelines from RBI, SEBI and ministry of company affairs with regards to transparency and disclosure.

Corporate compliance committee

Apart from mandatory committees, the company should frame corporate compliance committee.

Secretarial Audit

The Secretarial Audit should be conducted by a Company Secretary in Practice. The report on the audit of secretarial records shall be submitted by the secretarial auditor to the Corporate Compliance Committee of the Board of Directors of the company. The Secretarial Audit Report should form part of the Board's Report. The Audit partner/Firm should be rotated on the grounds as to maintain independence of Auditors and to look at an issue from different perspective. Corporate governance audits through selected corporate governance specialist who monitors effectiveness of corporate governance practices at companies.

Remuneration committee

The constitution of remuneration committee should be made mandatory.

Nomination Committee

By having a well functioning Nomination Committee, it will play a significant role in giving investors substantial comfort about the process of Board-level appointments. So the researcher recommends that listed companies should have a Nomination Committee. The constitution of nomination committee should be made mandatory.

Independent director

Independent director should be appointed as per existing guidelines. Clause 49 needs to be suitably amended by specifying positive attributes for independent directors such as integrity, experience and expertise, foresight, managerial qualities and ability to read and understand financial statements etc. Such independent directors should not be for name sake, but should be well aware of the company's progress, and should actively participate in the process.

The conduct of board meetings needs introspection in terms of frequency and duration, information needs, balance between presentation and discussion, interaction outside the boardroom and most importantly, consultation when in doubt. Independent directors need to conduct various exclusive sessions on a one-on-one basis with management, internal auditors and external auditors.

Stake holders value enhancement

There is a need to build and restore trust among stakeholders and improve the credibility in the independence of the board. In the context of meeting expectations of stakeholders beyond the minority shareholders (eg. employees, customers, suppliers etc.) a number of initiatives need to be embraced such as:

- Openness and transparency in dialogue with stakeholders

- ❖ Objective and transparent whistle blower policies that are available to key stakeholders (employees, customers and vendors) and provide adequate safeguards against victimization of whistle blowers.
- ❖ Have minority shareholders' representatives on boards as independent director.

Media as a stake holder

Capacity building in the area of corporate governance, has assumed critical importance in India, given the renewed emphasis on the subject in the light of the recent events. Media has an important part to play in raising general awareness and understanding of corporate governance and potentially as a watch dog in the area of corporate governance. Being a significant stakeholder itself, the media should consider upgrading capacity to carry out analytical and investigative reporting in matters impacting best in practice standards of corporate governance as they can play the role of a responsible and an effective stakeholder in protecting capital markets or securities markets from injury from corporate fraud. Further, the media, especially in the financial analytics and reporting business should invest more in analytical, financial and legal rigor and enhance their capacity for analytical and investigative reporting.

Effectiveness of Board

Boards should look upon the following views to be more effective:

- ❖ Board should demand and obtain a holistic view of risks both on and off the balance sheets, their ownership and how they are mitigated.
- ❖ Diversity of skills on the board is fundamental to effective risk management.
- ❖ The decisions of the board should be held keeping the best interest of company in view. The management should

realize that they are the trustees of the wealth assigned to them by the shareholders for social good rather than private profit.

In the ultimate analysis, it is an inner process of self-realization and enlightenment and not the outward imposed restrictions, code or stringent enforcement of regulatory framework.

Board systems and procedures

The board should undertake a formal and rigorous annual evaluation of its own performance and that of its committees and individual directors. Individual evaluation should aim to show whether each director continues to contribute effectively and to demonstrate commitment to the role (including commitment of time for board and committee meetings and any other duties). The chairman should act on the results of the performance evaluation by recognizing the strengths and addressing the weaknesses of the board. The board should state in the annual report how performance evaluation of the board, its committees and its individual directors has been conducted.

The Board and Committee Meetings should be facilitated to be attended through Tele-conferencing and video conferencing. E-presence of a director would ensure larger participation at Board/Committee meetings. The decisions may be subsequently recorded as a circular resolution signed by the directors physically present and those participating through audio or video-conferencing.

Audit committees

As per clause 49 guidelines, two-thirds of the members of the Audit Committee must be independent directors as must the chairman, but the rest may be either Non-Executive Directors or executive directors. But this is contrary to the Audit Committee and it must comprise entirely of non-executive directors with independent directors forming the majority. Some may also consider that the presence of executive directors on the audit committee needs to be appreciated since they are well versed with the internal working of the company and bring first hand information to the table which helps an objective and meaningful analysis of the discussions by the Committee.

Shareholder grievance committee

A share holder grievance committee is mandatory to exist for good corporate governance. The share holders are one of the major stakeholders in any company. Such a committee will not only help harmonizing the relationship but will also prove beneficial in other ways. If such committees do not meet the expected standards, then the share holder needs to actively participate in various other forms of confrontation.

Long term institutional investors, pension funds or infrastructure funds can help to develop a vibrant state of shareholder activism in the country. The oversight by such investors of corporate conduct can be facilitated through internal participation of their nominees as directors or external proceedings for preventing mis-management. Such institutional investors should establish model codes for proper exercise of their votes in the interest of the company and its minority shareholders, at general meetings, analyze and review corporate actions intended in their investee companies proactively and assume responsible roles in monitoring corporate governance and promoting good management of companies in which they invest.

Remuneration policy

Remuneration policy for the members of the Board and Key Executives should be clearly laid down and disclosed. Executive remuneration packages should involve a balance between fixed and incentive pay, reflecting short and long tern performance objectives appropriate to the company's circumstances and goal. The stock options should be invariably linked between the board performance and company performance.

Companies should ensure that the level and composition of remuneration is sufficient and reasonable and that its relationship to performance is clear. Incentive schemes should be designed around appropriate performance benchmarks and provide rewards for materially improved company performance.

Separation of the offices of the Chairman and the Chief Executive Officer (CEO)

Though there is no obvious causality between such a separation and better corporate governance or performance, it is nevertheless true that there is a growing trend internationally of separating the offices of the Chairman and the CEO. Most Indian listed companies are controlled by promoters and family groups, often holding over 50 per cent of the voting stock. Indeed, many in corporate India feel that the separation is not desirable — that the dominant, risk taking shareholder being both the Chairman and Chief Executive of a company gives a greater notion of commitment than otherwise. A counter argument is the absence of evidence supporting that separation of the two offices improves corporate performance or promotes good corporate governance practices. Further, separating Chairman & CEO provides no guarantee of better leadership and can add to a layer of potential conflict. Realizing the realities of India and keeping the culture in mind, it is recommended to separate the office of the Chairman from that of the CEO.

There should be a clear demarcation of the roles and responsibilities of the chairman of the Board and that of the Managing Director/ CEO. The Roles of Chairman and CEO should be separated to promote balance of power. A "comply or explain" approach should be adopted.

Corporate Social Responsibility

While setting the goals and objectives, a company must consider various expectations of the stakeholders into consideration. So companies should formulate strategies and take decisions that promote their economic goals as well as satisfy the social values at the same time. There also must be a regular review of the corporate goals to match the changing expectation of the society.

In order to gain confidence and trust of society, there should be transparent fair and adequate disclosure of social performance by the company.

Corporate social performance analysis and reporting should be wide spread, so that the levels of social performance and cost-benefit trade-offs can be better evaluated.

The corporate governance report should have a separate section wherein various steps and action taken by the companies towards their commitment of social responsibility are detailed in the form of a CSR report every year. Also there is a need for undertaking a social audit of the companies.

As per the researcher's findings, at least 0.2% of sales should be utilized for fulfilling corporate social responsibility.

The Legal and Regulatory Standards

All provisions should be aligned with the existing Listing Agreement and other SEBI legislations to achieve uniformity in corporate governance standards in the country. Yet due to the varying degree of best in practice standards for SMEs, listed companies and unlisted public companies, which have significant impact on the economy, it is suggested that regulations / prescriptions should be set under the Companies Law and its regulations from time to time and should be in synchronization with SEBI, as far as listed companies are concerned. For that purpose, joint committees of SEBI and the Ministry of Corporate Affairs should be constituted so that uniform, agreed upon standards are prescribed for listed companies under both laws.

Stringent provisions should be made to penalize companies which follow poor and unethical governance under the companies Act and SEBI guidelines. Such provisions should be implemented with utmost diligence.

Concerns regarding Corporate Governance

Monitoring mechanisms are weak in India as well as western countries. Such mechanisms should be strengthened and made evident in their role play. Principle based standards with moderate regulations and strong regulatory review mechanism will enforce corporate governance standards. This will put a brake on the frequent scams and frauds.

Information should be timely and well packaged to enable the decision making smooth and speedy.

The quality of management discussions and analysis of reports of companies should improve and on the basis of which the shareholders can make decision pertaining their investments.

Risk Management Framework

The sources of risk, and their magnitude, have changed dramatically and pose challenges not only to business and governments but also to society and economies. The board must be provided with information on the most significant risks and how they are being managed to integrate risk management in decision making activity. The Board, its audit committee and its executive management must collectively identify the risks impacting the company's business and document their process of risk identification, risk minimisation, risk optimization as a part of a risk management policy or strategy. The Board should also affirm that it has put in place critical risk management framework across the company, which is overseen once every six months by the Board.

Lock-in option

Remuneration of CEOs should be significantly linked to the company performance and involve a medium term "lock in" option.

Integrity and ethical values

- Striving to ensure that the code of conduct is understood and adhered to by all members of the organization
- The performance management system should recognize and reward ethical behavior
- Extensive background checks should be performed on the senior employees joining the organization
- Companies should screen third parties (customers, vendors, JV partners) with whom it does business for their commitment and adherence to ethical practices
- Investors, lenders, analysts should pro-actively question/challenge management on areas pertaining to corporate governance comprising protecting minority interests, management compensation, government dealing, risk management practices, related party transactions, fraud risk management and CSR.

Number of non-executive directors.

In case an individual is a managing or whole-time director in a listed company, the number of companies at which such an individual can serve as non- executive director, be restricted to 10, and the number of listed companies at which such an individual can serve as a non-executive director, be restricted to

3. The maximum number of listed companies in which an individual can serve as a director should be restricted to 6.

Investor Relations Cell

Constitution of Investor Relations Cell should be made mandatory for Listed Companies. The Investor Relations meet after declaration of financial results should be compulsorily webcast.

The role of the Audit Committee in related party transactions

Audit Committee, being an independent Committee, should pre-approve all related party transactions which are not in the ordinary course of business or not on "arms length basis" or any amendment of such related party transactions. All other related party transactions should be placed before the Committee for its reference.

Effective and Credible Enforcement

Multiplicity of investigating agencies leads to delay in the overall judicial process and possible misinterpretation of information. Regulators under the Company Law, the Securities Laws and the Serious Fraud Investigation Office should have an inter-se cooperation agreement. During the Harshad Mehta scandal, the Special Courts Act was empowered to consider both civil and criminal actions from the securities fraud transaction. A special bench of the Company Law Board or its successor, the National Company Law Tribunal should be invested with special powers for adjudication of civil recovery actions and for criminal offences and penalties to be levied there under.

So the instances of investigations of serious corporate fraud must be coordinated and jointly investigated. Joint investigations / interrogation by the regulators for example, the SFIO-Serious Fraud Investigation Office and the CBI should be conducted in tandem. On the lines of the recommendations of the Naresh Chandra Committee Report on Corporate Audit and Governance, a Committee should be constituted for each case under a designated team leader and in the interest of adequate control and efficiency, a Committee each, headed by the Cabinet Secretary should directly oversee the appointments to, and functioning of this office, and coordinate the work of concerned department and agencies. Civil recovery for acts of misfeasance, malfeasance, nonfeasance and recovery from the wrongdoers and criminal offences and penalties and punishments should be adjudicated appropriately, without conflicting reports and opinions, and disposed off between 6 to 12 months.

CONCLUSION

Capital Markets exerts an influential role on companies by imposing certain rules and regulations relating to firm's governance roles. Capital markets play a major role in and also impart some forces on both the sides. To reframe or understand the spectrum of fields of corporate governance, it becomes important to focus on listed companies in capital markets. The key to better corporate governance in India today lies in a more efficient and dynamic capital market. Markets play an invisible hand in imparting justice. The market appreciates well-managed companies and rewards them.

Corporate Governance has assumed great importance in the wake of frauds, scams as well as increasing competition and globalization. It stipulates parameters of accountability, control and reporting functions of the board of directors. It also emphasizes the proper relationship among various participants - the board, management, shareholders, banks, financial institutions, suppliers, creditors and the state – in determining the direction and performance of companies.

Tougher legal and regulatory provisions of corporate governance are required to check and prevent default by companies, as noted by the company secretaries' opinions. Such provisions should be implemented strictly as to bring about a positive change. So, apart from tough provisions, the larger issue is that of implementation. Since India is well known for its diversity and subtle acts, such implementation would be a mammoth task. In the study of 50 select blue-chip companies, 20 companies were not able to manage a respectable 60% compliance. Such appalling situation leads to the doubt if they would be able to implement the stringent rules and Acts of corporate governance.

Looking at the complexity of the situation, it is quite evident that only law cannot ensure good corporate governance without code of conduct and self- regulation. Laws, rules and regulations are required to strike a balance in the objectives sought to be achieved by different interest groups in companies, but the aim of corporate governance is commitment to values, business ethics and distinction between personal money and corporate funds.

The company secretaries' questionnaire survey shows that corporate governance's implementation should be enforced by laws and Acts, as well as a moral duty. The survey confirms that the major corporate governance concern in listed companies should be done to prevent controlling owners from expropriating minority shareholders. There is substantial room for improvement in recognizing the rights of shareholders. Shareholders are inadequately protected with such rights as priority capital subscription, approval of major related-party transactions, and dissenters' rights.

One fourth of the companies studied had too few independent directors as per guidelines. The functions of boards and board committees in the countries under review are generally weak. The boards seem to be somewhat inactive in selecting, monitoring, and replacing CEOs and reviewing the remuneration of key executives and directors. Outside or independent directors are inadequately supported with necessary and timely information. Over a half of the select companies did not meet with such compliance.

Corporate governance practices have been scored to come up with aggregate scores that can be used to investigate the link with company's financial performance. The scores are based only on practices related to transparency and disclosures, the effectiveness of boards, board systems and procedures and many other such parameters. Yet many of the companies who did not score high on such parameters, are financially sound, strong and well reputed in the market.

Even though the select companies under study may not embrace the guidelines wholeheartedly, the market obviously discriminates among companies, suggesting that companies will move toward meeting more of these guidelines. The study also provides evidence of a potential governance role in all parameters. The study indicates that the on-going corporate governance reform efforts should be continued to encourage companies to pay more attention to substance than to form. To enhance the effectiveness of boards, the provision of adequate support for outside directors seems to be the most important factor, as well as the promotion of a boardroom culture that encourages constructive criticism and alternative views. More broadly, as indicated by the respondents, priorities should be given to making internal corporate governance mechanisms work better and enhancing the standards for information disclosure, accounting, and auditing. Critically important for these tasks are the roles of regulatory agencies, independent directors, and professional associations and institutions, inclusive of professionals like statutory auditors and company secretaries.

Larger gaps and variations exist in areas where regulations and guidelines are less demanding or enforcement is difficult. For all the select companies there is clear evidence that corporate governance matters in the valuation of firms and that the market seems to be smart in evaluating the quality of firms' corporate governance, in that it tends to differentiate among firms more on the basis of substance than of form.

BIBLIOGRAPHY

1. Balasubramanian, N. (1993), 'Corporate Financial Policy', *Corporate Financial Policies and Shareholder Returns – The Indian Experience,* Himalaya Publishing House, New Delhi: 11.
2. Balasubramanian N. (2004), 'Approach to Company law Reforms', *Indian Institute of Management Banglore Management Review*: 14.
3. Balasubramanian, N. (2007), 'Control & Conflicts – Session 6', *IIM Bangalore Faculty Development Programme Notes*: 3.
4. Balasubramanian, N. (2007), 'Public Sector Governance – Session 19' *IIM Bangalore Faculty Development Programme Notes*: 50.
5. Baysinger, B. D. & Butler, H. (1985), 'Corporate governance and the board of directors: Performance effects of change in board composition', *Journal of Law, Economics, and Organization, 1:* 101–134.
6. Bhattacharyya, A. K. (2004), 'Issues in Corporate Governance in India', *Good*
7. *Governance, Democratic Societies and Globalization*, Sage Publications, New Delhi.
8. Birla Kumar Mangalam (2000), 'Corporate Governance Report', *The Chartered*
9. *Secretary*. BSE 30 Group Companies Details accessed on 1st June, 2010 from: http://www.bseindia.com.
10. BSE 200 Companies Details accessed on 10th April, 2009 from: http://www.bseindia.com.
11. Cadbury, Adrain Sir (1992), 'Report on Financial Aspects of Corporate Governance', *The Cadbury Committee Report.*

12. Chakrabarti, Rajesh (2005), 'Corporate Governance in India – Evolution and Challenges',*Working paper College of Management*, Georgia
13. Clive Smallman (2004), 'Corporate Governance & Ethics', *International Journal of Business Governance and Ethics* :Vol, 1, No. 1
14. CMIE (2006), 'Review of Indian Economy', *Monthly Review of Indian Economy,* Centre for Monitoring Indian Economy.
15. Cooke, T.E. and Sawa, E. (1998) 'Corporate Governance Structure in Japan: Form and reality', *Corporate Governance: An International Review*: 6(4), 217-223.
16. Corporate Governance Report (2004), SEBI report accessed on 24th February, 2007 from: http://www.sebi.gov.in/commreport/corpgov.html.
17. Corporate Social Responsibility Analysis accessed on 1st January, 2010 from: http://www.karmayog.org/csr2009/csr2009_29264.htm.
18. Dahya Jay, McConnell John and Travlos Nickolaos (2000), 'The Athens Laboratory of Business Administration', *The Cadbury committee Report.*
19. Das, S. C. (2005), 'Corporate Governance in Germany', *The ICFAI Journal of Corporate Governance.*
20. Das, S. C. (2005), 'Sarbanes Oxley Act (SOX) and its influence on Naresh Chandra Committee recommendations towards good corporate governance in Indian Corporates', *The Management Accountant.*
21. Das, S. C. (2009), 'Corporate Governance in India – A case study of selected listed companies for financial year 2004-05', *Corporate Governance in India – An Evaluation*, PHI Learning Pvt. Ltd.: 162-200.

22. Dombey, D. (2003), 'The Long March to Shareholder Democracy', *Financial*
23. *Times*.
24. Donaldson, L. and Davies, J.H. (1994), 'Boards and Company performances- Research challenges the conventional wisdom', *Corporate Governance: An International Review*: 151-160.
25. Egon Zehnder (2001), 'Board of Directors Global Study 2000', *Egon Zehnder International*.
26. Fama, E. F. & Jensen, M. C. (1983), 'Separation of ownership and control' *Journal of Law and Economics, 26:* 301–325.
27. Fernando, A.C. (1997), 'Corporate Governance: Time for a Metamorphosis,' *The Hindu.*
28. Fernando, A.C (2000), 'Corporate Governance: The Dire Need of the Hour', *Management Matters*: 1-7.
29. Fernando, A.C. (2009), 'Theoretical Basis of Corporate Governance', *Corporate Governance-Principles, Policies & Practices*: 46-47.
30. Fernando, A.C. (2010), 'Landmarks in the emergence of corporate governance', *Business Ethics and Corporate Governance*: 14.7
31. FICCI & GT (2009), *'Corporate Governance Review 2009: India 101-500 A review of corporate governance practices at the mid market listed companies in India'.*
32. Ganguly (2002), 'Consultative Group of Directors of Banks & Financial Institutions', *The Ganguly Committee Report*, Reserve Bank of India.
33. Gaur & Gaur (2006), 'Statistical Analysis', *Statistical Methods for Practice and*
34. *Research – A guide to data analysis using SPSS*, Sage Publication: 67-105.

35. Ghoshal Sumantra (2005), 'Bad Management Theories are Destroying Good Management Practices.' *Academy of Management Learning and Education*: 4(1), 75-91.
36. Gopalsamy, N. (1998), Corporate Governance The New Paradigm, Wheeler publication.
37. Greenbury (1994), 'Investigating board members' remuneration and responsibilities', *Greenbury Committee Report*.
38. Gupta, L.C. (17 March, 2004), 'Corporate Governance, Indian Style', *Economic Times*
39. Hampel (1998), 'Corporate Governance Regulations', *The Hampel Committee*
40. *Report.*
41. Hermalin, B.E. and Weisbach, M.S. (1998), 'The determinants of board composition', *Rand Journal of Economics*: 19, Winter, 589-606.
42. Hillman, A. & Dalziel, T. (2003), 'Boards of directors and firm performance: Integrating agency and resource dependence perspectives.' *Academy of Management Review, 28:* 383–396.
43. ICSI (2009), 'ICSI National Awards – Role of ICSI in promoting good corporate governance', *Corporate Governance – Modules of Best Practice,* ICSI New Delhi: 347-498.
44. IMS Health (2009), Global Pharmaceutical and Therapy Forecast, *Pharmaceutical Report.*
45. Irani, J. J. (2005), 'Report on Corporate Governance' accessed on 24th February,
46. 2008 from: http://dca.nic.in/report_expert_comt.htm
47. Jackling Beverley & Johl Shireenjit (2009), 'Board Structure and Firm Performance: Evidence from India's Top Companies', *Corporate Governance: An International Review, 2009, 17(4):* 492–509.

48. Jayanti and Subrate Sarkar (2000), 'Large Shareholder Activism in Corporate Governance in Developing countries: Evidence from India', *International Review of Finance*: Vol. 1, Issue 3.
49. Jensen Michael C. and Meckling William H. (1974), 'Theory of the Firm: Managerial Behaviour, Agency Costs and Ownership Structure', *Journal of Financial Economics, 3:* 303–360.
50. Joshi Vashudha (2004), 'Corporate Governance Models', *Corporate Governance - The Indian Scenario*, Foundation Books: 124 - 125
51. Keasey, K. and Wright, M. (1993), 'Issues in Corporate accountability and governance', *Accounting and Economics*: 24, 243-273.
52. Listed Companies Informations accessed on 1st July, 2010 from: http://nseindia.com.
53. Machold, S. and Casudevan, A.K. (2004), 'Corporate Governance Models in emerging markets: The case of India', *International Journal of Business Governance and Ethics*: Vol. 1, No. 1
54. Manikutty, S. (2005), 'Embedding CSR for Competitive Business Advantage' *The*
55. *Hindu Business Line*.
56. Monks, R.A.G and Minow, (2001), 'The New Global Investors: How Shareholders can Unlock Sustainable Prosperity Worldwide', *Capstone Publishing, Oxford.*
57. Monks R.A.G and Minow, (2010), 'International Corporate Governance', *Corporate Governance*, 4th Edition, Wiley India (P.) Ltd.: 351-410.
58. Murthy (2004), 'Corporate Governance Report', *Narayana Murthy Committee*
59. *Report.*

60. Narasimhan, C.R.L. (2004), 'Better Corporate Governance for stock exchanges',
61. *The Hindu.*
62. NASSCOM (2008), 'NASSCOM's Strategic Review 2008', *NASSCOM Reports.*
63. NASSCOM (2009), 'NASSCOM's Strategic Review 2009', *NASSCOM Reports.*
64. Nicholson, G. J. & Kiel, G. C. (2007), 'Can directors impact performance? A case- based test of three theories of corporate governance', *Corporate Governance: An International Review, 15:* 585–608.
65. Nunnaly, J. (1978), 'Cronbach Alpha Note', *Psychometric theory,* McGraw-Hill, New York.
66. Parkinson, J. E (1994), 'Corporate Power and Responsibility', *Oxford University*
67. *Press, Oxford.*
68. Principles of Corporate Governance, accessed on 26th March, 2009 from:
69. http://www.oecd.gov.
70. Ramsay, Ian and Geof Stapledon (2002), 'Corporate Governance: The Role of superannuation Trustees', *ICFAI Journal of Corporate Governance*: 72.
71. Rangarajan L.N. (1992), 'Kautilya, the Arthashastra English Translation', *Penguin Books*.
72. RBI (2009), 'Banking Industry ', *RBI Bulletin*.
73. Revised clause 49 (2003), SEBI circular (SEBI/MRD/SE/2003/26/08) accessed on 24th February, 2007 from: http://www.sebi.gov.in/circulars/2003/cir2803. html.
74. Roe Mark J. (2003), 'Political Determinants of corporate governance: political context', *Corporate Impact*.
75. Role of SEBI (2000), SEBI circular (SM/DRP/Policy/CIR-10/2000) accessed on

76. 24th February, 2007 from: http://www.sebi.gov.in/press/2000/200017.html.
77. Rosenstein, S. & Wyatt, J. G. (1990), 'Outside directors, board independence and shareholder wealth', *Journal of Financial Economics, 26:* 175–191.
78. Sanchez and Alfonso Vargas (1998), 'Agency Theory versus Stewardship Theory in Cooperative Societies', *Development of Corporate Governance Systems.*
79. Segmentation of Directors accessed on 1st July, 2010 from: http://directorsdatabase.com
80. Select Companies Annual Reports for FYs 2006-07, 2007-08 & 2008-09 accessed on October 2007 to October 2009 from: respective website of the select companies.
81. Seth, A. (2004), 'Corporate Governance Systems: An integrative Model and implications for India ', Sage Publications, New Delhi.
82. Shleifer, A. & Vishny, R. W. (1997), 'A survey of corporate governance', *Journal of Finance 52:* 759–783.
83. Solomon & Solomon (2007), 'A reference dictionary of corporate governance systems', *Corporate Governance and Accountability*, Wiley India (P.) Ltd.: 161-183.
84. Sreekumar, G. (2004), 'New Basel Norms to Change Complexion of Banking', *Business Review, The Hindu.* Srinivasachari C S (1994), 'European Settlements, The History and Culture of the Indian People', *Volume 7, The Mughal Empire*: endnote 5 to chapter XVI, 518.
85. Swami (Dr.) Parthasarathy (2010), 'Corporate Governance Concepts', *Corporate Governance, Principles, Mechanisms & Practice*.
86. Turnbull (1998), 'The Combined code of Best Practices in Corporate Governance.' *The Turnbull Committee Report.*

87. Varma, Jayanth (1997), 'Corporate Governance Problem in India', *Indian Institute of Management Banglore Management Review*: 9 (4), 5- 18.
88. Zysman, J. (1983), 'Governments, Markets and Growth: Financial Systems and the Politics of Industrial Change,' *Cornell University Press*.

www.ingramcontent.com/pod-product-compliance
Ingram Content Group UK Ltd.
Pitfield, Milton Keynes, MK11 3LW, UK
UKHW041939190726
13854UKWH00004B/1675